The Spanish
in America
1513 -1974

ETHNIC CHRONOLOGY SERIES
NUMBER 12

The Spanish in America
1513 -1974
A Chronology & Fact Book

Compiled and edited by

Arthur A. Natella, Jr.

1975
OCEANA PUBLICATIONS, INC.
DOBBS FERRY, NEW YORK

Library of Congress Cataloging in Publication Data

Natella, Arthur A
    The Spanish in America, 1661-1974.

    Ethnic chronology series : no. 12.
    Bibliography: p.
    Includes index.
    1. America--Discovery and exploration--Spanish.
2. United States--Civilization--Spanish influences.
3. Spain--Colonies--America. I. Title. I. Series.
E123.N37   973'.04'61   75-9887
ISBN 0-379-00511-5

Manufactured in the United States of America

TABLE OF CONTENTS

EDITOR'S FOREWORD

In the Western Hemisphere the two most important languages are English and Spanish. The latter is the mother tongue of approximately 175 million Americans -- a figure that outstrips any other. In the United States alone, some 5 million people use Spanish in their daily lives.

Our country is well acquainted with the exploits of conquistadores who followed Columbus to the New World -- Cortés, Pizarro, Balboa, Ponce de León, de Soto and Coronado, to name but a few. However, to specific questions asked concerning the contributions that Spain first, then later our Spanish-speaking neighbors to the South have made to our nation, the answers frequently betray hesitation and even uncertainty. Not well known is the influence that the Hispanic nations have had upon our architecture, literature, music, and our history.

The Hispanic heritage is profound. Six of our States - Florida, Texas, Montana, California, Colorado and Nevada have Spanish names. So do hundreds of mountains, rivers, towns, villages, and even cities. The architecture, language, and flavor of the American Southwest were creations of Hispanic people. One might say that our cowboys inherited their trade, attire, and jargon from the Spaniards.

One of the most accepted objectives of history is to explain what is important in the present. Hence, in an attempt to introduce to its readers the background and foundation for the Spanish motif that exists in art, music, movies, fashions, literature, etc., as well as to proudly identify the varied roles that people of Hispanic origin have played in the development of our country, this little volume is fondly added to the others of the Ethnic Chronology Series.

In an attempt to give a representative picture of the contribution of the Hispanic culture to North America may it in some small way, at least, help to erase narrow-mindedness, prejudice, and intolerance, and in their place nurture a healthy spirit of understanding and brotherhood.

Arthur A. Natella Jr.
University of Maryland

CHRONOLOGY

1513   April 2. The former governor of the Island of Puerto Rico,
                Ponce de León, landed on the southern coast of Florida on
                Easter Sunday or Pascua Florida.

1519   Alonso de Pineda explored the Gulf Coast of the United States
                as far west as present-day Texas, showing clearly that
                North America was a continent.

1521   Francisco Gordillo y Quexos reached the coast of North
                Carolina.

1523   Lucas Vásquez de Ayllón was named Adelantado or repre-
                sentative of the Spanish crown, in a vast unsettled region
                north of Florida.

1525   Esteban Gómez explored the Atlantic Coast from Florida to
                Labrador, passing the mouths of the Connecticut, Hudson,
                and Delaware rivers, a region known on old Spanish maps
                as Tierra de Gómez (Land of Gomez).

1526   Lucas Vásquez de Ayllón founded San Miguel de Guadalupe,
                the first European settlement in North America.

                Pánfilo de Narváez was given the right to explore, conquer,
                and settle that region of Spanish territory extending from
                Florida to the Río de las Palmas (Rio Grande).

1527   Pánfilo de Narváez set out to explore the region from Flor-
                ida to the Rio Grande. Only four men were to survive the
                mission: Alvar Núñez Cabez de Vaca, Alonso Castillo, An-
                drés Hurtado, and their slave, Esteban. The group crossed
                the American Southwest on foot, landing in the Gulf of Cali-
                fornia in 1554.

1538-1539   Francisco de Ulloa explored the Gulf of California.

1539   Fray Marcos de Niza explored the American Southwest
                reaching the present state of New Mexico.

1539-1541   Hernando de Soto landed at Tampa Bay and explored a vast
                area including Florida, Georgia, South Carolina, Alabama,
                Mississippi, and Arkansas. The expedition consisted of
                600 soldiers and 213 horses. Most notable, perhaps, among
                the accomplishments of this expedition was the discovery
                of the source of the Mississippi River.

1540   February 22. Francisco Vásquez de Coronado led an ex-
                pedition of 250 soldiers and 800 Indians through parts of
                Arizona, New Mexico, Colorado, Texas, and Kansas. One of
                Coronado's representatives, López de Cárdenas, is credited
                with the discovery of the Grand Canyon in Arizona.

                Hernando Alarcón explored the Colorado River.

                The horse was introduced on a large scale in the United
                States by Spanish explorers.

1542-1543   Juan Rodríguez Cabrillo and Bartolomé Ferrelo explored
                the Pacific Coast of the United States from San Diego Bay
                to Oregon; this expedition was the first to set foot on the
                Pacific Coast of the United States.

1550-1600   Spanish explorers were instrumental in introducing new
                crops and livestock into North America. Pigs, cattle, poultry,
                rabbits, sugar cane, wheat, oats, barley, and rye were intro-
                duced from Europe.

1559   Spanish settlers founded Pensacola, Florida.

1565   Spanish settlers founded St. Augustine, Florida, the first
                permanent European community in North America. It was
                here that the first Catholic parish within the limits of the
                present-day United States was founded by Fr. Don Martín
                Francisco López de Mendoza Grazales, chaplain of the Span-
                ish settlers in the area.

1566   The first Jesuit mission in North America was founded in
                Florida.

                An expedition led by Juan Pardo left the settlement of Santa
                Elena (South Carolina) and reached as far north as North
                Carolina.

1567   Pedro Menéndez de Avilés became Florida's first governor,
                ruling until 1574.

1570   By this date, Jesuit missionaries had established a mission
                in the Chesapeake Bay.

1573   Pedro Márquez explored the Chesapeake Bay.

1582   Antonio de Espejo, a rich Mexican merchant, led an expedi-

tion into New Mexico, which he called New Andalucia, after
the name of Spain's southernmost province.

1597   Sebastián Vizcaíno sailed from Acapulco with three ships
        to explore the Sea of Cortes and the Gulf of California.

1598   Juan de Oñate explored the area north of the Rio Grande,
        reaching as far north as Missouri and Nebraska. During
        this journey, the expedition performed what is considered
        the first theatrical work presented within the present limits
        of North America. During the expedition, at least two plays
        were performed, one written by Captain Marcos Farfán de
        los Godos and another called Los moros y los cristianos.
        Subsequently, Juan de Oñate became New Mexico's first
        governor. His administration lasted until 1608.

1602   Under orders of Philip III of Spain, Sebastián Vizcaíno un-
        dertook another expedition to map the coast of California.
        He reached as far north as the 43rd parallel.

1603   Martín de Aguilar explored the coast of Alaska.

1610   A member of Juan de Oñate's expedition, Captain Gaspar
        Pérez de Villagra, wrote an epic poem about the explora-
        tion of New Mexico, La historia de la Nueva Mexico, later
        published in Alcalá, Spain.

        The Palace of Governors was constructed in Santa Fe, New
        Mexico.

1630   By this date Spanish settlers had instituted at least twenty-
        five missions with fifty Franciscan friars in New Mexico.
        At these missions workshops and schools were set up for
        the instruction of the Indians.

1661   Diego Dioniso Peñalosa Briceño was appointed governor and
        captain-general of New Mexico.

1672   Spanish settlers in Florida began construction on a defen-
        sive edifice called the Castle of San Marcos. This construc-
        tion, which had taken about twenty-five years to complete,
        was declared a national monument in 1942.

1680   An Indian uprising in New Mexico led to the virtual abandon-
        ment of frontier settlements in this area until 1696.

1683   The first permanent settlement in Texas was made by the
        Spanish.

1686   Alonso de León explored Texas, founding the first mission in that area, San Francisco de los Tejas.

1687   A Spanish friar of Austrian descent, Eusebio Kino, founded the Dolores Mission, the first of a large number of Jesuit missions in southern Arizona.

1699   The preacher Cotton Mather wrote the first book to be published in Spanish in the United States: La religión pura en doze palabras fieles, dignas de ser recibidas de todos.

1706   Spanish settlers founded the city of Albuquerque, naming it after the viceroy of Mexico, the duke of Albuquerque.

1716   Texas was separated from Coahuila and was created as a separate Mexican province.

1720   Father Margil de Jesús founded the Mission of San José and San Miguel de Aguayo in the San Jose Valley of Texas. This beautiful edifice has been considered by many art historians as the finest example of baroque architecture in North America.

   Martín de Alarcón was appointed the first governor of Texas.

1722   The famous Texas fort, the Alamo, was constructed as a Franciscan mission.

1741   The first grammar book of the Spanish language in the United States was published in New York by Garret Noel. It was entitled A Short Introduction to the Spanish Language.

1745   An early history of Texas was written by Franciscan fathers who wrote on missionary activities as well as on the language and culture of the Indians.

1748   Jacob Rodríquez Rivera settled in Newport, Rhode Island, after an early career in Curacao. This wealthy merchant introduced the sperm oil industry to the colonies and is said to have introduced the manufacture of spermaceti candles as well.

1751   The first sugar cane grown in North America was introduced into Louisiana by missionaries from Santo Domingo.

1762   France under Louis XIV ceded its colony of Louisiana to

Spain to prevent it from falling into British hands. Spain did not actually take over the administration of Louisiana until 1765. During its existence as a colony of Spain, Louisiana was under Cuban administration. In 1810, by the Treaty of San Ildefonso, Spain receded Louisiana to France, which took possession of the colony in 1803.

British forces briefly occupied Havana.

1763   As a result of the Treaty of Paris, Spain ceded part of Florida to England in return for Cuba.

1764   Cuba became a separate captaincy-general within the Spanish overseas empire, controlling the Louisiana and Florida territories held by Spain.

1766   The Spanish government united the territories of Texas, New Mexico, Arizona and the northern states of Mexico under the name Las Provincias Internas.

1767   Pedro Fages, first comandante of Alta California and later governor, was born.

1768-1774   The Spanish missionary-explorer Francisco Tomás Hermenegildo Garcés, assigned to the Mission San Xavier del Bac, made four expeditions to points on the Gila and Colorado rivers.

1769   Alarmed at finding that Russians had crossed the Bering Strait, King Carlos III of Spain ordered the founding of missions on the Pacific Coast. In this year the first expedition was sent northward from Mexico to establish a mission at San Diego, in honor of San Diego of Alcalá. This was the first mission founded in Alta California. Don Pedro Fages and Gaspar de Portolá were the first white men to discover the San Francisco Bay. On their second trip, they discovered Monterrey Bay and established the Mission San Carlos de Borromeo at present-day Carmel, California.

1771   Fray Junípero Serra founded the Mission San Gabriel Arcángel in a valley not far from the present city of Los Angeles. This friar was instrumental in the construction of a large number of missions and is often considered the chief guiding force behind the success of the Spanish missions in the Southwest and in California.

1774   Captain Anza and Father Garcés along with twenty soldiers established a land route between the American Southwest and California after numerous other attempts to establish such a route had failed. This discovery led to the later development of San Francisco.

1774-1775   Juan Pérez and Francisco de la Bodega explored the coast of Alaska.

1775-1776   Silvestre Vélez de Escalante explored Arizona and Colorado, becoming the first white man known to travel in Utah.

1776   The College of Philadelphia offered the first college course in the United States on Spanish grammar and literature.

              Spanish missionaries under Fray Junípero Serra founded the Dolores Mission at the center of present-day San Francisco.

              Carlos III of Spain sent 4 million silver reales to aid the North American revolutionaries in their struggle against Great Britain.

1777   Arthur Lee, representative of the American government, met in Spain with banker Diego Gardoqui and the Marquis de Grimaldi. An agreement was made by which the Spanish government would send aid to the American colonists. Gardoqui later came to the United States where he corresponded for a time with President George Washington.
              During the Revolution, Spanish ports offered refuge to American ships. In addition, arms and financial support for the American revolutionaries were sent from New Orleans and Cuba to the fighting forces.

              December 31. A Cuban, Juan de Miralles, left Cuba to establish a diplomatic liason between the government of Spain and the Congress of Philadelphia.

1780   Bernardo de Gálvez, governor of New Orleans, lent active support to the North American rebels in their battle against England.

1781   The city of Havana sent financial aid to the rebellious American colonists, thus helping Washington launch important battles toward the end of the revolution.

1783   Juan Manuel de Cacigal, governor of Cuba, wrote to General Washington supporting his revolutionary efforts, calling him the Fabius of his day.

After twenty years of British occupation, East Florida was returned to Spanish hands by the Treaty of Versailles.

The famed Latin American Francisco de Miranda came to the United States, meeting American dignitaries and attending lectures at Yale University. Accordingly, he has been considered the first Latin American student in the United States.

1786   Pedro Vial began planning the Spanish trail, a route designed to link San Diego and St. Augustine, Florida.

1789   Alejandro Malaspina began further explorations of the Pacific Coast of the United States.

1791   The Spanish introduced sugar cane to Louisiana, and in this year they established the first sugar refinery in New Orleans.

1795   February 27. José Antonio Navarro, a distinguished Mexican-American, was born. On January 18, 1960, Governor Price Daniel of Texas proclaimed February 27 as Navarro Day in Texas in honor of Navarro, a signer of the Texas Declaration of Independence who later served on the committee that wrote the 1836 Texas constitution and who subsequently served in both the Texas Congress and Senate.

1797   What has been considered the most impressive of the colonial buildings in California, the main church of the Mission of San Jaun Capistrano, was begun. It was completed in 1806 and was designed by Isodoro Aguilar.

1802   One hundred merino sheep, the first in the United States, were brought from Spain by Col. David Humphreys, U.S. Minister to Spain.

1803   France, under Napoleon Bonaparte, regained control of the former Spanish Louisiana Territory.

1804   The Mission of Santa Inés was established by Spanish settlers; this was to be the last mission to be founded in Southern California.

The United States annexed by force the Territory of Western Florida.

1815   Upon his death, Abiel Smith endowed Harvard University with funds to establish the Smith Chair of Spanish, a prestigious position, later held by George Tickner, Longfellow, and George Lowell among others.

1819   The Adams-Onís Treaty ceding Spain's Florida holdings to the United States was signed.

1821   Texas came under the control of the newly established Empire, and later Republic, of Mexico.

Spain granted Moses Austin land in Texas for settlement.

Spain ceded the remainder of its Florida territory to the United States.

1823   The Cuban poet José María de Heredia came to reside in the United States where, greatly impressed by the violent beauty of Niagara Falls, he composed his well-known Ode to Niagara, which appeared in The United States Review and Literary Gazette, edited by the poet William Cullen Bryant.

The last Spanish mission in Alta California was founded in Sonoma.

1824   Conductor, composer and impressario Jaime Nuñó was born in San Juan de las Abadesas, Spain. Nuñó later came to live in the United States where he was active as a performer and teacher.

1825   Italian opera was introduced to New York on a regular basis at the Park Theater with Il Barbiere di Siviglia. The cast was led by the famous tenor Manuel García.

1829   Miguel Antonio Otero was born in Valencia, New Mexico. Otero, who studied law at St. Louis University, was a member of New Mexico's House of Representatives from 1852 to 1854. He became attorney general of the Territory of New Mexico in 1854 and was a Democratic Congressional Representative from 1856-61. In 1861 he was appointed acting governor of New Mexico by President Lincoln.

1830   The Mexican government passed the Colonization Law, which encouraged the migration of Mexicans into Texas.

1831   The Mexican-American Estevan Ochoa was born. Ochoa was instrumental in the development of the first public school system in the Arizona territory. He later served also as a member of the territorial legislature and mayor of Tucson.

1835   Texas proclaimed its independence from Mexico.

1836   Based on a study of land grants and other historical docu-
               ments, it has been shown that a number of Mexican-Ameri-
               cans took part in the American defense of the Alamo.

1839   Poet, essayist, novelist, and playwright Thomas Cooper de Leon
               was born in Columbia, South Carolina. It is said that his play
               Hamlet Ye Dismal Prince (1870) was the first American play
               to run 100 nights.

1843   Henry Wadsworth Longfellow, a lover of Spanish letters
               and a translator of many of the Spanish classics, finished
               his play The Spanish Student, a work that follows the theme
               of Cervantes's novelette La gitanilla.

1845   The Mexican government sent Captain Andrés Castillero
               on a military mission to Fort Sutter, where he discovered
               the New Almader quicksilver mine. This discovery of quick-
               silver, which is essential in the process of separating me-
               tal from waste in the mining of gold and silver, made pos-
               sible the later mining of these metals in California.

               Between 1845 and 1846, the Los Angeles-born Pío Pico be-
               came the last of thirteen governors who administered Cali-
               fornia during the twenty-four years of Mexican rule.

1846   July 7. United States annexation of California was pro-
               claimed at Monterrey after the surrender of the Mexican
               garrison.

1847   Domingo Faustino Sarmiento, the distinguished Argentine
               statesman and writer, arrived in the United States. Sar-
               miento traveled widely, forming a friendship with the edu-
               cator Horace Mann and with his wife, who subsequently was
               the translator of Sarmiento's biography of Lincoln. In much
               of Sarmiento's writing there is an accent on inter-American
               relationships. His Rhode Island Speech is considered the
               first attempt by an American of either hemisphere to de-
               scribe the relations between the Hispanic and Anglo-Saxon
               cultures. Sarmiento, who later became president of the
               Argentine Republic, received an honorary degree from the
               University of Michigan.

1848   By the Treaty of Guadalupe-Hidalgo, Mexico formally recog-
               nized the North American claim to Texas and ceded New
               Mexico and Alta California to the United States.

1849   Cirilo Villaverde, the author of the classic of Cuban fiction,
               Cecilia Valdés, visited the United States for the first time
               this year. During his stay in New York he continued his

literary and journalistic efforts on behalf of the cause of
the Cuban patriots. He was editor of the journals La Verdad
and El Espejo and contributed to other reviews such as Las
Américas and The Frank Leslie Magazine. Villaverde subsequently died in New York in 1894.

1850   Msgur. José Alemany Sadoc, a catalonian priest, became
the first Spanish bishop of Monterrey, later becoming arch-
bishop of San Francisco.

The name of the State of California was derived from the
Spanish literary work, Las Sergas de Esplandián (1510) by
Garci Ordóñez de Montalvo. Among the many other American place names of Hispanic origin are the names of the
states of Colorado, Nevada, and Florida.

By this date the cattle-raising tradition of the American
Southwest clearly showed its origins in the Hispanic tradition. The American cowboy himself is often considered to
be a hybrid developed from the Anglo-American settler, the
Spanish landowner, and the Mexican vaquero. The cowboy
saddle was essentially an adaptation of a traditional Spanish-
style saddle that the Spaniards had, in turn, borrowed from
the Moors. In California, ranching disputes were often settled by the "rancheros," or meetings involving one or more
judges. This tradition seems to be a continuation of the
Spanish Alcaldes de la Mesta.

Much of the vocabulary of the cattle business was derived
from Spanish words. Among many examples are the following: rodeo, corral, burro, latigo, hacienda, lasso, pinto, palo-
mino, vammose(vamos) dolly welter(dar la vuelta), stampede
(estampida), calaboose(calabozo). In addition, many geo-
graphical terms common in the Southwest had a common
Spanish origin, for example; mesa, sierra, canyon, and tor-
nado.

1853   Under provisions of the Gadsden Purchase, the United States
acquired Southern Arizona and the New Mexican territories
from Mexico at a price of $10 million.

Venezuelan pianist and composer Teresa Carreño was born.
Miss Carreño, considered one of the world's greatest pian-
ists, was the teacher of Edward MacDowell, one of America's
most important composers.

Ernesto Francisco Fenellosa, a poet and student of Oriental
art, was born. After teaching political economy and philoso-
phy in Japanese universities, he became the curator of the department of Oriental art at the Boston Museum in 1890. Fenellosa was a well known expert on Oriental art, and it has
been said that he discovered the subject for the American
art world.

1854   The Colombian poet Rafael Pombo was sent to New York as
            secretary to the Colombian legation. He remained there for
            five years, during which time he composed poems in English,
            several of which were published by William Cullen Bryant
            in the New York Evening Post.

1859   Octaviano Larrazolo, jurist, senator, and governor of New
            Mexico, was born in Allende in southern Chihuahua, Mexico.
            Larrazolo, who was a strong champion of the rights of the
            Mexican-Americans, was New Mexico's first governor after
            World War I (1918), and in 1928 he was elected to the United
            States Senate.

1865   Chilean writer and statesman Benjamín Vicuña Mackenna
            founded La voz de América in New York, the first periodi-
            cal dedicated to promoting the unity of the Americas. This
            writer, besides being the author of several travel books,
            including one about his stay in North America, wrote several
            volumes on the subject of inter-American relations.

1866   David G. Farragut, son of Jorge Farragut, was appointed
            to the rank of admiral in the United States Navy. In 1862
            and 1866 Farragut received a vote of thanks from the United
            States Congress for his distinguished naval service to the
            Union during the Civil War, especially in sea battles at
            Mobile and New Orleans.

1866   Alexander Del Mar was named director of the Bureau of Sta-
            tistics.

1869   Arístides Agramonte, the noted Cuban bacteriologist, was
            born. He was a member of the American Academy of Sci-
            ences and a member of the United States Army board that
            discovered the transmission of yellow fever by mosquitoes.

1879   Alonso Garcelon was elected Democratic governor of Maine.

1880   José Martí, Cuban patriot and writer, came to New York
            where he lived until 1895. Martí contributed frequently to
            New York newspapers, notably The Sun.

1882   The American architect Henry Richardson toured Spain in
            this year. During his trip the buildings he saw made a deep
            impression on him, particularly the Cathedral of Salamanca.
            This influence can be seen in American buildings such as
            Trinity Church in Boston and the Albany Cathedral. The in-
            fluence Richardson exerted on other American architects
            of the period was great. In fact, it is said that he set an
            architectural pattern that dominated the eastern United
            States from 1880 to 1893.

1883   Columbia College of Columbia University introduced the first course in Latin American history in the United States. It was taught by Daniel de León.

1884   Spanish opera singer María Barrientos was born in Barcelona. In 1916 she came to the United States and made her debut at the Metropolitan Opera House in New York in the role of Lucia. She was also a pianist, violinist, and composer, having completed a symphony while still only a child.

Spanish sculptor José de Creeft was born. He came to the United States in 1929 and became a naturalized citizen in 1940. He was given numerous showings in some of America's finest museums, including exhibitions at the World's Fair in New York in 1964 and the White House Festival of the Arts in 1965. He has also completed murals, mosaics, and sculpture, which can be seen in New York City.

1885   The American painter James Whistler declared in an address his admiration and indebtedness to Spanish painters, noting especially the influence of Velásquez in his portrait of the violinist Saraste.

1898   The Spanish-American War broke out after the battleship Maine exploded in the harbor of Havana. By the Treaty of Paris, Spain granted independence to Cuba and ceded Puerto Rico, Guam, and the Philippines to the United States in return for a payment of $20 million.

The artist Xavier González was born in Spain. González later came to the United States where he has been represented in many of the country's best museums and where he received an award from the American Academy of Arts and Letters.

1899   Actor Ramon Novarro was born. An important star in the history of film, he appeared in dozens of motion pictures over a period of more than thirty years.

1900   Xavier Cugat, the popular violinist and conductor, was born. Cugat, who made his first appearance with the Cuban Symphony Orchestra at the age of six, toured the world as an accompanist for Enrico Caruso. Later he formed his own orchestra, which has played in prominent hotels and night clubs throughout the United States.

1901   Pablo Casals, the famous cellist, composer, and conductor,
made his first concert tour of the United States. Subsequently, Pablo Casals visited and lived in this country in
his capacity as performer, teacher, and conductor.

1903   November 18. The Hay-Bunau-Varilla Treaty gave the
United States control of a ten-mile strip of land in Panama
at the cost of $10 million and a yearly payment of $250,000.

1904   The United States Supreme Court ruled that citizens of
Puerto Rico are not aliens and may not be denied admission
to the continental United States.

The sculptor José de Rivera was born in New Orleans. His
work can be found in collections in major museums throughout the United States.

The Hispanic Society of America was founded in New York.

1906-1913   Approximately 8,000 Spaniards were brought into Hawaii
as agricultural workers.

1907   Cesar Romero was born. This movie actor, the grandson
of Cuban patriot José Martí, has enjoyed a career as a distinguished show business personality.

1910   Admiral Horacio Rivero was born in Puerto Rico. Admiral
Rivero, who has enjoyed a distinguished naval career, is
currently commander-in-chief of Allied forces in southern
Europe.

1912   The famous Spanish singer Lucrezia Bori made her Metropolitan Opera debut in the title role of Manon Lescaut, opposite Enrico Caruso. Renowned as one of the great prima
donnas of the Metropolitan Opera, she gave guest appearances and concerts all over the world. After her retirement
in 1936, she became the first woman to serve on the Metropolitan's board of directors.

The Chilean abstract artist Roberto Sebastián Matta Echaur-
ren was born. Trained as an architect in Santiago and in
Paris under Le Corbusier, he was an active member of the
surrealist movement and a friend of Marcel Duchamps.
During the Second World War he came to live in New York
in the company of other famous artists such as Max Ernst,
André Masson, and Yves Tanguy; he was considered a

strong influence on the growth of American abstract expressionism.

The famous Puerto Rican actor José Ferrer was born.

1913   Permanent civil government was established in the Panama Canal Zone by executive order.

The Alamo was restored as a patriotic monument by authorities in San Antonio, Texas.

1914   August 15, the Panama Canal was formally opened.

The Cuban-American pianist Jorge Bolet was born in Havana. Since coming to the United States, he has enjoyed a distinguished career. Among other honors, he received the Joseph Hofmann award for outstanding artistry in 1938. In 1968 he was named professor of music at the Indiana University School of Music. Among his many credits, Mr. Bolet performed the piano soundtrack for the film Song Without End, the story of the life of Franz Liszt.

José García Villa, a Philippine poet of Spanish descent, was born in Manila. He later came to the United States where he wrote poetry and prose and has been the recipient of important literary prizes and fellowships. He is generally considered to be the first-ranking Philippine poet writing in the United States.

1915   The famous screen star Anthony Quinn was born in Chihuahua, Mexico.

1916   Juan Ramón Jiménez, the famous Spanish poet and winner of the Nobel Prize for Literature, visited the United States for the first time. Later the poet took up residence in the United States where he taught at several American universities. His collection Romances de Coral Gables (1948) reflects his stay in North America.

Angel Reyes, the Cuban-American concert violinist, was born. Mr. Reyes made his Carnegie Hall debut in 1941 and became a naturalized citizen of the United States in 1955.

The distinguished Spanish scholar Federico de Onís came to the United States as a professor of Spanish at Columbia

University. In 1920 he became director of the newly founded
Hispanic Institute at the same university. For many years
de Onís became not only the guiding force behind the study
of the Hispanic culture at Columbia University, but also
one of the most eminent Hispanic scholars in the United
States.

1917   Argentine actor Fernando Lamas was born. He has appeared
              successfully in numerous films since 1950.

              Noted actor and director Mel (Melchor) Ferrer was born
              in Elberon, New Jersey.

1919   Spanish author Blasco Ibáñez's novel The Shadow of the Ca-
              thedral was published in New York. The distinguished
              American writer William Dean Howells, the so-called fa-
              ther of American realism, wrote the introduction, in which
              he commented with embarrassingly lavish praise that the
              novel was one of the best in modern literature, superior to
              any written in English up to that time. Howells had corres-
              ponded with the Spanish novelist Armando Palacio Valdés
              and states in his book Criticism and Fiction that this author
              was a strong influence on his own concept of realism.
                   In 1878, Howell's play Yorick's Love, an adaptation of
              Un drama nuevo by the Spanish playwright Manuel Tamayo
              y Baus, was presented in Cleveland.

1920   The well-known actor Ricardo Montalban was born in Mexi-
              co.

              Actress, singer, and dancer Margo (María Margarita Guada-
              lupe Bolado y Castilla) was born in Mexico City. She made
              her film debut at fifteen in Paramount's Crime without Pas-
              sion. Since then she has been active in films, stage, night
              clubs, television, and radio. Among her film credits are
              Lost Horizon (1937), I'll Cry Tomorrow (1955), and Who's
              Got the Action? (1963).

1921   The Spanish artist Federico Castellón came to the United
              States where he has enjoyed great success with his numer-
              ous one-man shows in important museums and galleries.

1923   Juan Oró, a Spanish scientist now living in the United States,
              was born. In 1955 he joined the faculty of the University of
              Houston. In 1967 he was appointed principal investigator
              for NASA lunar sample analysis.

1924   The noted theatrical director José Quintero was born in
              Panama City, Panama.

              The noted Spanish historian and critic Américo Castro came
              to the United States as a visiting professor at Columbia Uni-
              versity. He later held the Emory Ford Chair of Spanish at
              Princeton University.

              The distinguished Mexican-American Ralph Guzman was
              born. Mr. Guzman served as a consultant to Secretary John
              Gardner of the Department of Health, Education and Welfare
              and to Secretary Robert C. Weaver of the Department of
              Housing & Urban Affairs on the problems of the Mexican-
              Americans in the United States. Dr. Guzman was also as-
              sociate director of the United States Peace Corps for the
              Republics of Venezuela and Peru.

1925   The popular band leader Tito Puente was born in New York
              City.

              The famous Spanish poet and dramatist Federico García
              Lorca arrived in New York to study at Columbia University.
              Poeta en Nueva York, an important collection of poems, was
              a result of his stay in the United States. A bilingual edition
              of these poems was published in New York in 1940.

1927   The Mexican painter José Clemente Orozco came to New
              York where he exhibited Drawings of the Revolution at the
              Mary Harriman Gallery. During the next nine years he com-
              pleted three famous mural series: those at Pomona College
              in Claremont, California (1936), for which he painted his fa-
              mous Prometheus; those at the New School for Social Re-
              search in New York (1931); and those at Dartmouth College
              in Hanover, New Hampshire (1932-34).

              The famous philosopher George Santayana (Jorge Augustín
              Nicolás de Santayana) published The Realm of Essence, the
              first of an important four-volume treatise of philosophic in-
              quiry, The Realms of Being.

1928   José Iturbi, the great Spanish pianist, gave his American
              debut. In addition to serving as guest conductor for many of
              America's leading orchestras, he was musical director of
              the Rochester, New York, Philharmonic Orchestra between
              1935 and 1944 and was named musical director of the Bridge-
              port Symphony in 1967.

The distinguished Spanish ophthalmologist Ramón Castro-
viejo came to the United States, becoming a naturalized citizen in 1936.

Flamenco dancer José Greco came to the United States,
soon becoming a naturalized citizen. He toured the country
during the years 1943-45 and since then has given countless
recitals in the United States, establishing an international
reputation in his field.

1929   Royes Fernández, the distinguished ballet dancer, was born
            in New Orleans in this year.

1930   The Chilean ballerina Lupe Serrano (Guadalupe Martínez)
            was born in Santiago. After making her debut in the Palacio
            de Bellas Artes in Mexico in 1943, she came to the United
            States and became a member of the American Ballet Theatre
            in 1953; she is currently prima ballerina and has appeared
            in numerous lead roles of important works in the ballet re-
            pertoire.

            The noted Puerto Rican pianist Jesús María Sanromá, who
            has given numerous concert appearances in the United
            States, joined the faculty of the New England Conservatory
            of Music.

1931   Puerto Rican actress Rita Moreno was born. She has been
            an actress-dancer in motion pictures since 1950, appearing
            in such films as Pagan Love Song (1950), The King and I
            (1956), and West Side Story (1961).

            The Mexican artist Diego Rivera was invited to come to
            New York where the Museum of Modern Art organized an
            exposition of his work. He painted frescoes in Rockefeller
            Center (never completed or destroyed), San Francisco, and
            Detroit.

1932   Boxer Kid Chocolate became featherweight boxing champion.

            Fashion designer Oscar de la Renta was born in the Dominican
            Republic. He came to New York and became fashion designer
            for Elizabeth Arden. He later opened his own establishment,
            Oscar de la Renta, Inc.

1935   Mexican mural painter David Alfaro Siqueiros opened a
            workshop in New York for experimenting with materials
            suitable for mural painting.

Conductor Jorge Mester was born in Mexico in this year. He later came to the United States where he studied with Leonard Bernstein among others, becoming a citizen in 1968. He has been a faculty member at the Juilliard School of Music and has been the musical director and conductor of many major American symphonic orchestras.

1936 The Spanish poet and critic Pedro Salinas took up residence in the United States, teaching at Wellesley and Johns Hopkins University.

1937 Trini Lopez, the popular Mexican-American singer and entertainer, was born.

1938 Desi Arnaz, the Cuban actor and producer, is credited with introducing the conga dance in the United States during his appearances in Miami in this year. He was musical director for Bob Hope and has been extremely active in television and movies since then.

The famous Spanish film director Luis Buñuel worked as director of documentaries for the Museum of Modern Art in New York City. In 1940 he became supervisor of Spanish-language versions of films for M-G-M studios. In recent years Buñuel's films have become very popular with American audiences.

1939 The noted Spanish architect and city planner José Luis Sert came to the United States and became a naturalized citizen in 1951. Since then he has received innumerable honors and distinctions in his field. He was a professor of city planning at Yale University from 1944-45 and dean of the Graduate School of Architectural Design at Harvard University from 1953-69. He has designed important buildings at Harvard University and Boston University.

1940 By official count, native Spanish-speaking Americans in the United States were numbered at 1,811,400. Unofficial estimates, however, ran as high as 4,000,000.

The famous Spanish artist Salvador Dali came to the United States.

Chilean-born Armando Zegrí, author and journalist for the National Broadcasting Company, reported World War II as a correspondent from the Pacific Theater and subsequently served as a UN information officer in Japan and Korea.

Opera singer Martina Arroyo was born in New York.

Anaïs Nin, an American writer of Spanish-French descent, came to the United States after a long stay in Europe. Upon her return she began her career as a major novelist.

Spanish novelist Ramón Sender came to the United States where he became professor of literature at the University of New Mexico.

1942 Spanish neurophysiologist José Manuel Rodríguez Delgado was appointed professor of medicine at the Yale University School of Medicine.

1943 The Mexican muralist Rufino Tamayo completed mural decorations for the library of Smith College in Massachusetts.

1944 Juan Zurita was named lightweight boxing champion after his defeat of Sammy Argott.

1945 The Cuban ballerina Alicia Alonso started her first season with the American Ballet Theatre. Since then she has become a major figure in the world of dance with innumerable appearances to her credit.

1946 President Truman named Jesús T. Piñero governor of Puerto Rico. He was the first Puerto Rican to occupy the post.

1947 The Spanish artist Juan Miró came to the United States where he designed a mural in the Terrace Plaza Hotel in Cincinnati.

Mexican actress Dolores del Río (Lolita Dolores Martínez Asunsolo López Negrette), a popular Hollywood star, made her last American film, John Ford's The Fugitive.

1948 Spanish musician Carlos Montoya came to the United States.

Richard (Pancho) A. Gonzalez won the men's singles lawn tennis championship.

1949 The Spanish writer José María Ferrater Mora came to reside in the United States where he has taught at leading universities such as Princeton and Johns Hopkins.

1950 Actor José Ferrer won an Academy Award for his portrayal of Cyrano de Bergerac.

1952   Puerto Rico became a commonwealth of the United States.

1954   María Antonita Martínez, an American craftsman, has won numerous awards for her creative work, including a decoration of the palmes academiquia by the French Ministry of Education, awarded in this year.

     Beatriz Bermejo Moore, together with the Spanish singer Lucrezia Bori, established the first private organization for Hispanic culture, the Spanish Institute, Inc. of New York.

1955   Musicians Joe Mondragon (bass) and Chuck Flores (drums) contributed to the development of so-called West Coast jazz.

     Celso Ramón García, born in New York in 1921, was appointed Sidney Graves Fellow in gynecology at Harvard University. In 1961 he was recipient of the Carl G. Hartman award for medical research.

1958   The Argentine composer Lalo Schiffrin came to the United States. Since then he has received numerous awards including the Grammy award in 1966. He has composed for more than fifty films and television shows.

1959   Alex Olmedo won the men's indoor tennis championship in the singles division, also winning in this year the Wimbledon championship in the men's singles division.

     A Spanish scientist living in the United States, Severo Ochoa, won the Nobel Prize for medicine for his work on the synthesis of RNA and DNA.

     President Eisenhower presented the Spanish artist Juan Miró with a $10,000 Guggenheim International Art Award for his mural Night & Day.

1960   Reporter Andrew López of United Press International was awarded the Pulitzer Prize for photography.

     The Mexican dancer José Arcadio Limón was awarded the degree of honorary doctor of fine arts by Wesleyan University. Mr. Limón, who has lived in the United States, has been a dancer and choreographer for numerous Broadway shows and has been on the faculty of a number of American colleges and universities.

1961   Baseball player Orlando Cepeda became the National League
                home-run champion.

                Henry B. González was elected congressional representative
                from Texas in the twentieth district.

                Joseph J. Jova was appointed United States ambassador to
                Honduras. In 1965 he was appointed permanent United States
                representative to the Organization of American States.

1962   Carlos Ortiz became the lightweight boxing champion.

                Cuban-American pianist Horacio Gutiérrez emigrated to the
                United States, becoming a citizen in 1967.

                Emilio Núñez was appointed justice of the Supreme Court
                of New York City. Since 1969 he has been associate justice
                of the appellate division of the New York Supreme Court.

1963   Luis Rodríguez became the welterweight boxing champion.

                Rafael Osuna won the U.S.L.T.A. tennis championship.

                Sugar Ramos became the featherweight boxing champion.

1964   Raúl Héctor Castro was named United States ambassador
                to El Salvador. In this same year he was the recipient of
                the D.A.R. Outstanding Citizen Award.

1965   Manuel Santana won the U.S.L.T.A. National Tennis Cham-
                pionship.

                Joseph M. Montoya was elected U.S. Senator from New
                Mexico.

                The Cuban musician and composer Chico O'Farrill returned
                to New York after a stay in Mexico where he wrote his First
                Symphony for performance by the Havana Symphony Orches-
                tra. In recent years he has lived in the United States where
                he has contributed to the success and popularity of Latin
                American music.

                Ismael Laguna became the lightweight boxing champion.

                José Torres became the light-heavyweight boxing champion.

                José Feliciano began to establish himself as a popular en-
                tertainer.

Eligio de la Garza was elected congressional representative from Texas's fifteenth district.

Daniel Fernández was the first Mexican-American to win the Congressional Medal of Honor.

Professor Alvo M. Camacho of the University of Tennessee and Efraín Toro-Goyco were awarded the Lederle Medical Faculty awards as distinguished scientific researchers

The artist Carlota Gonzales was commissioned, along with her husband, to design the mural for the War Memorial edifice in Honolulu.

1967   The Washington Opera Company presented the world premiere of the opera Bomarzo by the Argentine composer Alberto Ginastera.

A fifty-foot steel sculpture by Pablo Picasso was presented at Chicago's Civic Center.

Architect Jorge Sanín Arango was selected by the Architectural Record as the creator of the best designed residence in the United States during this year.

The Argentine actor Alejandro Rey became a naturalized citizen in this year. He has appeared in numerous motion pictures including Tea and Sympathy (1955), Five Finger Exercise (1958), and Impulsion (1970).

1968   Luis A. Alvarez was awarded the Nobel Prize for physics.

The golf star Lee Trevino was the first golfer to score four sub-par rounds in U.S. Open competition. He is also co-holder of the all time low scoring record in U.S. Open competition.

1969   Jockey Jorge Velásquez was named top money winner of the year.

Anthony J.P. Farris was appointed U.S. attorney for the Department of Justice in Region VI.

Herman Badillo was elected congressional representative from New York State's twenty-first district.

Manuel Luján Jr. was elected congressional representative from New Mexico's first district.

1970   President and Mrs. Nixon invited the popular Mexican-American singer Vikki Carr (Florencia Bisenta de Casillas Martínez Cardona) to entertain at a White House state dinner in honor of President Rafael Caldera of Venezuela.

Rev. Patrick Flores became the first Mexican-American to be named a Roman Catholic bishop in the United States.

1971   Jim Plunkett, the Mexican-American football star, was named rookie of the year of the American Football Conference by United Press International.

Lee Trevino teamed up with Jack Nicklaus to win the sixty-eighth national World Cup Golf Tournament at Palm Gardens.

Baseball player Joe Torre received the National League's most valuable player of the year award.

Samuel Zachary Montoya was appointed justice of the New Mexico Supreme Court.

1972   Mrs. Romana Acosta Bañuelos was named treasurer of the United States.

1973   Puerto Rican baseball great Roberto Clemente was elected to Baseball's Hall of Fame after his tragic and untimely death in December of 1972.

Argentine musician Gato (leandro) Barbieri established himself in the United States as a popular composer and musician.

Phillip Victor Sánchez was named U.S. ambassador to Honduras.

The Spanish government established a fund of $587,000 toward the completion of a $1 million, 140-yard Spanish-style plaza in New Orleans. The plaza was suggested by Luis Aparicio, the Spanish consul in New Orleans, as a commemoration of Spain's part in the history of Louisiana.

Golfer Chi Chi Rodríguez won the Greensboro Open golf tournament.

1974   Fernando E.C. de Baca, western regional director of the
              U.S. Department of Health, Education and Welfare, was
              named special assistant to President Nixon for Hispanic af-
              fairs.

              Rev. Robert F. Sánchez was appointed archbishop of the
              diocese of Santa Fe, New Mexico.

DOCUMENTS

THE TREATY OF TORDESILLAS
1494

Signed on June 7, 1494, the Treaty of Torde-
sillas moved the line of demarcation of Spain's
discoverable territory 370 leagues west from
the Cape Verde Islands.

Source: Henry Steele Commager, ed., Docu-
ments of American History, eighth edition, p.4.
New York: Appleton-Century-Crofts, Inc., 1968.
Copyright 1968 by the Meredith Corporation.

. . . Whereas a certain controversy exists between the said lords, their constituents, as to what lands, of all those discovered in the ocean sea up to the present day, the date of this treaty, pertain to each one of the said parts respectively; therefore, for the sake of peace and concord, and for the preservation of the relationship and love of the said King of Portugal for the said King and Queen of Castile, Aragon, etc. it being the pleasure of their Highnesses, they . . . covenanted and agreed that a boundary or straight line be determined and drawn north and south, from pole to pole, on the said ocean sea, from the Arctic to the Antarctic pole. This boundary or line shall be drawn straight, as aforesaid, at a distant of three hundred and seventy leagues west of the Cape Verde Islands, being calculated by degrees. . . . And all lands, both islands and mainlands, found and discovered already, or to be found and discovered hereafter, by the said King of Portugal and by his vessels on this side of the said line and bound determined as above, toward the east, in either north or south latitude, on the eastern side of the said bound, provided the said bound is not crossed, shall belong to and remain in the possession of, and pertain forever to, the said King of Portugal and his successors. And all other lands, both islands and mainlands, found or to be found hereafter, . . . by the said King and Queen of Castile, Aragon, etc. and by their vessels, on the western side of the said bound, determined as above, after having passed the said bound toward the west, in either its north or south latitude, shall belong to . . . the said King and Queen of Castile, Leon, etc. and to their successors.

Item, the said representatives promise and affirm . . . that from this date no ships shall be dispatched—namely as follows: the said King and Queen of Castile, Leon, Aragon etc. for this part of the bound . . . which pertains to the said King of Portugal . . . nor the said King of Portugal to the other side of the said bound which pertains to the said King and Queen of Castile, Aragon, etc.—for the purpose of discovering and seeking any mainlands or islands, or for the purpose of trade, barter, or conquest of any kind. But should it come to pass that the said ships of the said King and Queen of Castile . . . on sailing thus on this side of the said bound, should discover any mainlands or islands in the region pertaining, as abovesaid, to the said King of Portugal,

such mainlands or islands shall belong forever to the said King of Portugal and his
heirs, and their Highnesses shall order them
to be surrendered to him immediately. And
if the said ships of the said King of Portugal
discover any islands or mainlands in the
regions of the said King and Queen of
Castile . . . all such lands shall belong to
and remain forever in the possession of the
said King and Queen of Castile . . . and
their heirs, and the said King of Portugal
shall cause such lands to be surrendered

immediately. . . .

And by this present agreement, they . . .
entreat our most Holy Father that his Holi-
ness be pleased to confirm and approve this
said agreement, according to what is set
forth therein; and that he order his bulls in
regard to it to be issued to the parties or
to whichever of the parties may solicit them
with the tenor of this agreement incorporated
therein, and that he lay his censures upon
those who shall violate or oppose it at any
time whatsoever. . . .

EVIDENCE OF THE MERITS AND SERVICES OF JUAN DE CÉSPEDES
1568

Source: Charles Wilson Hackett, ed., Historical
Documents Relating to New Mexico, Nueva Vizcaya,
and Approaches Thereto to 1773, p. 47. Washington, D.C.: Carnegie Institution of Washington,
1923. Courtesy of the Carnegie Institution of
Washington.

*Evidence of the merits and services of Juan de Céspedes in the exploration
and conquest of the new land of Cíbola, where he went with Governor
Francisco Vásquez Coronado, and in the uprising in New Spain.
Mexico, January 19, 1568.*

I. *Sacred Catholic Royal Majesty.* Captain Juan de Céspedes affirms
that he has served your Majesty in New Spain more than thirty years,
since the time when Don Antonio de Mendoza and Don Luís de Velasco
were governors of it, and afterwards the royal Audiencia, afterwards the
Marqués de Falces, afterwards the licentiate Alonso Muñoz, and Doctor
Luís Carillo of your royal Council, and Don Martín Enríquez,[20] who
governs for your Majesty at present, up to this year of '75; and that he
has served on all occasions that have presented themselves in that land,
even in the affair of the uprising and rebellion which occurred in it. In all
that time he has served your Majesty as your captain and by governing
as your *corregidor* and *alcalde mayor* in the best and most important
provinces in the kingdom, in Spanish cities as well as in native, winning
for himself the confidence that was required. All of which appears more
at length in the reports and proofs which he has made and presented in
your royal Audiencia of New Spain and in your royal Council of the
Indies, with the titles which he has of having been your captain and having
practised in your name the said duties and offices. And your royal Council of the Indies has ordered it placed in the memorial. His services and
merits have been and are very well known. . . . December 7, 1575.

ANTONIO DE ESPEJO ELECTED AS LEADER
1582

A relation of the election of Antonio de Espejo
as leader of the expedition into New Mexico,
1582-1583.

Source: George P. Hammond & Agapito Rey,
eds., Expedition into New Mexico Made by
Antonio de Espejo 1582-1583, pp. 63-64. Los
Angeles: The Quivira Society, 1925. Reprinted
by Arno Press, Inc., 1967.

As we had no chief to lead and govern us we assembled and elected from among ourselves one of the
companions called Antonio de Espejo, as captain and
chief magistrate, in the name of his majesty the king
Don Philip our lord, whom may God preserve. We took
the oath of fealty to him, as is stated in the commission
which we gave him. Thus we began to prosecute the
said expedition.

We left this place of San Bernardino on the seven-
teenth of the month of December, going up the river
named Del Norte, to serve God our Lord and his
majesty and to bring succor to the friars. This Rio del
Norte we named El Rio Turbio because it is exceedingly
muddy; it always flows northwest. We followed it all
the time, leaving it sometimes at a distance of a league,
but we always stopped along it for the night except when
by some pools formed by the freshet. It is a river that
flows through a plain. It flows so quietly that it does
not make any noise in spite of being very large in some
places. It is three leagues in the widest part when it
becomes swollen. It is such a river that all of these
three leagues [in width] are covered with numerous

groves of poplars and willows, there being in it very few willows or any other sort of trees. It is inhabited by naked people like the Otomoacos. These people always received us peacefully. In spite of this, however, and the fact that we always took along some of their people from one ranchería to another, we were on our guard and very cautious in watching our camp and stock.

A RELATION OF THE EXPEDITION OF ANTONIO DE ESPEJO
1582-1583

Source: George P. Hammond & Agapito Rey,
eds., Expedition into New Mexico Made by
Antonio de Espejo 1582-1583, pp. 86-92.
Los Angeles: The Quivira Society, 1925. Reprinted by Arno Press, Inc., 1967.

*They met friendly Indian mountaineers who brought
them maize.*

We left this place on the second of the month and
marched two leagues to a marsh which extends from a
mountain. We found here peaceful Indian mountaineers who brought us tortillas even though we did not
need them as we had abundant provisions. We named
this place La Ciénaga Deseada del Pinal.

We set out from this locality on the fourth of the
month and marched four leagues. We camped at a
large lagoon where a small river disembogues. It
originates along the route from Sumy thereto.

*They learned of the people of Ácoma and went there.
It is situated on a high rocky hill, with flights of steps.*

We learned that close to this place was a pueblo called
Ácoma. So we left the camp by this lagoon and Captain Antonio de Espejo, Diego Pérez de Luxán, and six
other companions went to the pueblo of Ácoma which
was four leagues distant from this place. Because of
the war this pueblo has with the Querechos Indians, who
are like the Chichimecos, it is built on a high rocky cliff.

It has four ascents made of steps carved in the very rock
and up which one person at a time can climb on foot.
The doors of the houses are like trap-doors. They keep
watch day and night.

They came to meet them with great rejoicing and merri-

ment.   They were given many blankets, tanned deer-
skins, turkeys, and much maize.

The natives came out to meet us and in order to honor
us they performed a very impressive dance after the
Mexican fashion, in which women took part, wearing
Mexican blankets, very elegant with paintings, feathers,
and other trappings.   There they gave us many blankets,
tanned deerskins, turkeys, and much maize.

They found many irrigated fields of maize with canals
and dams as if built by Spaniards.

We left the aforesaid place on the seventh of the
month and marched four leagues up a river which originates in some bad lands.   We found many irrigated
maize fields with canals and dams as if Spaniards had
built them.   We stopped by the said river and named
this place El Rio de San Martín.

We set out from this locality on the eighth of the
month and marched four leagues.   We halted at a place
one league and a half beyond the spot where the river
flows into a marsh, which we named El Salitrar.

We left this place on the ninth of the month and
marched four leagues.   We camped at some bad lands
without water.   It snowed so much that we were
forced to halt in this place.

We departed from this place on the tenth of the
month and went seven leagues and came to a large pine
forest.   We slept on the mountain because it snowed
so much that we were unable to proceed.   We retired
without water, and this day drank snowwater melted in
pots and pans.   We named this place El Elado.

We set out from this place on the eleventh of the
month and marched three leagues and stopped at a water-
hole at the foot of a rock.   This place we named El
Estanque del Peñol.

We left this place on the thirteenth of the month, I

mean the twelfth, and marched seven leagues. We
camped at a small arroyo with water, and because there
was a very high rock in the shape of a sugar loaf we
named this site El Real del Pilón.   Here at the request
of the party two aides to the captain were chosen,
Gregorio Hernández and Bernaldino de Luna.   They
granted, in the name of his majesty, the office of *alférez
mayor* to Gregorio Hernández, and to Diego Pérez de
Luxán that of *alguacil mayor* of the camp and of the new
gobernación of New Andalusia and of the first town or
city that should be founded, with a vote in its cabildo.

*They found the province of Zuñi and six pueblos called
Mazaque, Quaquema, Aguico, Alona, Quaquina, and
Cana.   Poor people.*

We set out from this place on the fourteenth of the
month and marched a league.   We halted at the first
pueblo of the province of Zuñi which they called
Malaque, in which we had a row of houses [for our use],
and they gave us to eat of what they had until we went
to other neighboring pueblos.   The people of this
province, which comprised six pueblos, one of which is
called Mazaque, another Quaquema, another Aguico,
another Alona, another Quaquina, and another Cana,
are poor, because even though they wear the same sort
of dress as the others the blankets are of agave fibre,
as the land is cold, for they gather little cotton.   The
women wear their hair done up in large puffs.

*They found crosses, all well built, because Coronado and
Chamuscado had been there, as the Indians stated.
They found here Mexican Indians and some from
Guadalajara, brought by Coronado.*

We found very well built crosses †† in all these
pueblos, because Coronado had been in this land, and also
throughout the land discovered by Fray Agustín and

Francisco Sánchez Xamuscado. Everywhere they told
us he had been there. Here we found Mexican Indians
and also some from Guadalajara, of those that Coronado
had brought. We could understand them but they
spoke with difficulty. Here we found a book and a small
old trunk left by Coronado.

*Report of mines; the people of these provinces are in-
dustrious and peaceful; they are good farmers and the
soil productive; houses of stone, mostly of whetstone,
three and four stories high.*

We got news of mines, and so God being pleased we
are going to discover them. I shall give an account of
whatever takes place. I merely wish to say that if there
are good mines this will be the best land ever discovered,
because the people of these provinces are industrious and
peaceful. There are many mountains and lands for
cultivation; for they are great farmers. The houses are
all of stone, mostly of whetstone, three and four stories
high.

*They went to another pueblo named Aguico where they
stayed from March 15 to April 7; lodged in good
houses and supplied with hares and rabbits.*

From this pueblo we went to another called Aguico
which is four leagues from the first one in this province.
We stayed here until the seventh of April, lodged in some
houses and provided with abundant hares and rabbits.
This was the time for planting their fields as it was
Easter. There were as many mists as if it were in the
midst of winter, for most of the showers in this land
come in the form of snow.

It seems that the natives have an estufa for every
fifteen or twenty residents, built under ground with
heavy timbers and roofed; all lined with slabs in such a
way that they keep so warm that in the coldest weather

they are naked, and they sweat here in these estufas.
The Indians spin cotton and weave blankets. They say,
however, that they obtain part of this cotton in trade
from the province of Mohose, which is a temperate
land. The blankets which the men and women wear
are of agave [yucca] fibre, so well carded that it re-
sembles flax.

*The people are pure Mexicans in everything; very in-
dustrious.*

Men and women are pure Mexicans in walking, in
crying, and even in their dwellings, but neater than the
Mexicans. They are very industrious.

We learned from the interpreters that two captains of
Coronado were in this pueblo two years and that from
here they went to discover provinces and that when
Coronado was at Puala de los Mártires, where the friars
had been killed, he came to the above-mentioned pueblo
of Ácoma, made war on them, and they surrendered.

There he was informed that the Tiguas, who are Puala
people, and their district had killed ten horses of the
ones which Coronado had left there for the people
in the garrison. When Coronado heard about it he left
for Puala, whose [people] are Tiguas, and besieged
them near a pueblo in a circular sierra. He pressed
them so hard that those who did not die at the hands of
the Spaniards, whom the natives called Castillas, for thus
they called Coronado's men, died of hunger and thirst.
Chamuscado and his men were not ignorant of this.
They knew it all, but they did not wish to say so in order
that some might come to settle the land. Finally the
people of Puala surrendered and put themselves at his
mercy. He required the service of the necessary Indians,
men and women, and returned to this pueblo. From
here he set out for the valley of Samora, which must be

one hundred leagues distant from this province.

*The people of these provinces are healthy, as they did
not see any cripples or sick, but only many old people.*

In this pueblo, about one-fourth of a league away,
there is a large marsh with many waterholes so that they
irrigate some fields of maize with this water.   There
are two canals with water and ample space to build a
city or town, as there are many mountains and good
lands.   They are extremely healthy people, for neither
in this province nor in the others we have crossed have
we seen any sick or crippled people, except many old
ones.

RELATION OF THE TRIP TO THE ERBELA (CÍBOLA) CATTLE
UNDERTAKEN BY THE SERGEANT MAJOR
on September 15, 1588.

Here Juan de Montoya gives an account of a
Spanish expedition into the Southwest.

Source: George P. Hammond & Agapito Rey,
eds., New Mexico in 1602, Juan de Montoya's
Relation of the Discovery of New Mexico,
pp. 50-54. Albuquerque: The Quivira Society,
1938. Reprinted by Arno Press, Inc., 1967.

On September 15 there set out from the camp the
sergeant major Vicente de Zaldívar Mendoza, the pur-
veyor general Diego de Valdibias, Captain Aguilar, and
other captains, and upward of six hundred soldiers.
They were well furnished with many droves of mares and
other necessities for handling cattle. They reached Pecos,
from which they set out on the 20th, leaving there as
prelate of that province Father Francisco de San Miguel
of the order of St. Francis, and Juan de Dios, a lay
brother versed in their language.

After traveling four leagues they came to a place on the
bank of the river where there are countless cattle. Two
leagues beyond they found water, although they retired
that night without any. In the morning they marched two
leagues farther, coming to a small river with little water
but abundant fish, such as voga, sardines, shrimps, and
mataloto.   With only one hook a large number were
caught that night and the following day.

Four vaquero Indians came out at that place, and they
were given good food and gifts. One of them rose and
shouted to many Indians who were in hiding, and they all
came to meet the Spaniards. They are robust people and

excellent archers. The sergeant major gave presents to everyone, reassured them, and asked them for a guide to go to the cattle which they furnished gladly. On the following day they traveled six leagues and came to some rainwater. At this place three Indians came out from a ridge, and, being asked where their ranchería was, they replied it was a league away and that they were very much disturbed by our presence in the land. In order that they might not be frightened further at the sight of many people, the sergeant major, with a single companion, went to their ranchería and told the three Indians through an interpreter why they had come.

We came to a very large river which flows from the east toward Florida. We all believed it to be the Madalena, which flows into the said Florida. These Indians have this custom of asking for something: they stretch the palm of their right hand toward the sun and then turn it toward the person whose friendship they seek. The sergeant gave them presents in this fashion. They importuned him to visit their ranchería. And although it was near sunset he had to go, lest it might appear to them that he did not do it on account of fear. He went thither and visited with the Indians in great friendship, and returned to his camp long after dark. On the following day while on the march many Indians, men and women, came to meet them. Most of the men go about naked, some wear skins, and a few of them blankets. The women wear some sort of chamois breeches, and shoes and boots after their custom.

He presented them with some trinkets and told them through the interpreter that he had been sent by the governor, Don Juan de Oñate, to tell them he would help them, and that they should remain loyal to his Majesty, and that he would punish those who were not. They were all pleased and reassured and asked for help against

the Xumanos, a nation of Indians streaked [painted]
like the Chimeros [Chichimecos]. The sergeant major
promised them peace and urged them all to keep it, for
to this end he had come to their land.

Taking leave of them he departed, and in the following
three days they traveled ten leagues. Near some marshes
they saw more than three hundred cattle. In three more
days they marched seven additional leagues and came
upon four thousand head of cattle. At that place there
was a fine location to set up a corral, and after they had
started to build it the cattle moved more than eight
leagues inland.

The sergeant major with ten soldiers proceeded to a
river six leagues away. There came from the direction of
the province of the Picures, and the Sierra Nevada, a
place indicated by the guide, a large number of cattle that
live in the sierra. When the party reached the river the
cattle had withdrawn because many vaquero Indians, who
were returning from trading with the Pecures and other
populous pueblos of this New Mexico, had crossed. To
these pueblos they sell meat, hides, tallow, lard, cotton,
and maize.

The sergeant passed the night in that locality and, on
the following day, as he was returning to camp, he came
upon a ranchería. It was composed of five hundred tents,
made of extremely well dressed hides, red and white.
They were round shaped, like pavilions, with buttons and
holes, as they are made in Italy. They were very neat and
so large that the average one could easily accommodate
four mattresses. The dressing is so excellent that water
will not go through, even in a downpour, nor will the
leather harden. On the contrary, when it dries it becomes
white and pliable as before. This being so amazing, the
sergeant major wanted to try it himself. Cutting a piece
of hide from one of the tents, he soaked it in water and

dried it in the sun, and it remained as soft as if it had not been wet. The said sergeant major bought a complete tent and took it along. Despite its being so large, as has been said, it did not weigh over two arrobas.

To transport this burden and the poles which they use to set it up the said Indians employ some medium-sized woolly dogs. They serve them as mules, and they often have a large pack of them, girt around the breast and on the sides and carrying loads of at least four arrobas. It is very amusing to see them on their way, dragging the ends of the poles, most of them with sores from the harness, make their journey one behind the other.[38] To load them they hold the head between their legs. In this manner they load them and straighten the load, for seldom is it necessary to come near them again since they travel at a pace as if they had been trained with fetters.

Back at the camp they rested that day and the following, as it was the day of St. Francis; on October 5 they traveled to find the main body of the cattle, and in three days they covered fourteen leagues. They found the cattle and killed a large number of them. On the next day they went three leagues farther on in search of a suitable place and facilities for a corral. They located a place and then proceeded to build one with large logs of cotton-woods. It took them three days to complete it. They made the wings so ample that they expected to inclose therein ten thousand head, because, during those days, they saw so many and they came so close to the tents and the cavalcade. In view of this and that when they run they seem to jump as if they were crippled, they considered the prey very easy. Furthermore, it was affirmed that in that place alone there were more than in three of the most populous ranches of New Spain put together, according to those who have seen them all.

ARTICLES OF AGREEMENT BETWEEN THE VICEROY
AND DON JUAN DE OÑATE, 1595

Source: Charles Wilson Hackett, ed., Historical
Documents Relating to New Mexico, Nueva Viz-
caya, and Approaches Thereto to 1773, pp. 265,
267, 279, 271. Washington, D.C.: Carnegie
Institution of Washington, 1923. Courtesy of the
Carnegie Institution of Washington.

*The articles of agreement which the viceroy, Don Luís de Velasco, made
with Don Juan de Oñate, governor and captain-general of the provinces of New Mexico, in accordance with the royal ordinances for
such discoveries, together with the modifications of the viceroy,
the Count of Monterey, and with the advantages that follow from
the confirmation of the articles of the viceroy, Don Luís, and the disadvantages brought with them by the modifications made by the said
Count of Monterey. [1595?]*

1. Article.   Item: That I shall have the power to recruit men in any
part of the kingdoms of his Majesty for the settlement and pacification,
naming for it the captains and necessary officials, raising banners, beating
drums, and proclaiming the expedition, as is provided in article 73 of the
ordinances.

Ordinance 73.   Let cédulas be issued granting power to raise men in
any part of these our kingdoms of the crown of Castile and León for the
settlement and pacification, and to name captains for it, to raise banners,
to beat drums, and to proclaim the expedition, without anything being
required for them or of those who may go upon it.

Modification.   The power to raise men shall not be general nor permanent, but for this occasion only.   And when they are used up, or more
are necessary, let permission be asked of the viceroy, as was granted to
Urdiñola.

The naming of officials of war shall not be for as long a time as he
may wish but for this time only and with consultation, as was granted to
Urdiñola.   And if the favor should be granted him, this from now on
shall be understood to be for the time that he may be subject to the charge
of the viceroys of New Spain, for if he were not it would be contrary to

their authority for captains and officials to be named by another and for people to be raised in it [New Spain].

Advantages of article 1. For an expedition of such great importance it is very necessary to be able to raise men whenever they are required, as it conduces to the greater service of his Majesty that the governor shall have authority in his name to be able to raise men at his choice and will, for it would thus be in his power to select those qualified and experienced and expert in such conquests of the Indies, as is necessary, and at the same time [to choose them] for the confidence that must be felt in each one where it is necessary for the soldiers to be as experienced and expert as their own captains and officers of war. For those [wars] which are had with the Indians are very different from others, for, since the number of the Indians is so far in excess of that of the Spaniards, everything is done by tricks and stratagems; therefore it is necessary that the soldiers shall be men of courage and valor, that they shall expect much reward, and that they shall be chosen by the governor who is in immediate charge of the conquest and is a witness of its occurrences, and who is so far away from the viceroy of Mexico that recourse to him is most difficult. For exactly the same reasons the governor ought to have the power to name the officials of war, whereby he can reward those who have to take part in it and those who work the best in it. If this is not done many errors are to be feared in the choice of such officials, and especially if they are dependents of the said viceroy, without the governor having power to appoint them or to remove them when he sees and learns that they are filling their offices badly or that they are not fit for them.

Disadvantages of article 1, modification. That the viceroys shall provide with supplies those who go at their own choice and those whom the *oidores* wish to go, their servants and relatives, for they thus take away the places from the deserving and from those who have the means to make the expedition and to take others who might also make it; the favorites of the viceroys and ministers are always necessitous and have to be aided with everything. The worst thing is what happened to Don Juan, who sent for men to help him, and because he had to wait until the viceroy, the Count of Monterey, gave permission for it to be done, ten months passed before the relief went, and at last it did not number one hundred men, which is the reason why nothing is known of Don Juan or his army since March 2, 1599, when the last reports and letters were received from him.

2. Article. Item: That after I have entered upon my said government and have taken possession of it, I shall have the power to choose and name

a royal treasury and royal officials, treasurer, *contador, factor,* and the others who may be necessary for the said royal treasury, with a suitable salary, the said salary to be paid from the property that will belong to his Majesty in the said government.   Let it be granted what is ordered in articles 43 and 64 of the said ordinances.

Ordinances 43 and 64.   When the land, province, and place has been chosen in which the new settlement is to be made, and investigation made of what supply of provisions may be in the possession of the governor in whose district it may be, or upon whose district it borders, let it be declared whether the pueblo that is to be settled is to be a city, town, or village.   And in conformity with what is declared let the council of the commonwealth and the officials and members of it be established, as it is stated in the book of the commonwealth of Spain shall be done; so that, if it be a metropolitan city, it shall have a judge with the title and name of *adelantado,* or governor, or *alcalde mayor,* or *corregidor,* or *alcalde ordinario,* who shall have universal jurisdiction and together with the *regimiento* shall have the administration of the commonwealth.   [In addition there shall be] three officials of the *real hacienda,* twelve *regidores,* two executive clerks, two jurymen, and in each parish one attorney, one *mayordomo,* one clerk of the council, two public clerks, one of mines and registry, one chief town crier, one *corregidor de lonja,* and two constables.   And if it be diocesan or suffragan it shall have eight *regidores* and the other said officials perpetually.   For the towns and villages there shall be an *alcalde ordinario,* four *regidores,* one *alguacil,* one clerk of the council and public clerk, and one *mayordomo.*   If there are no officials of the *real hacienda* power shall be given to name and provide them in the interval until we shall provide them or until those whom we have provided go.

Modification.   That the power to name royal officials with a salary shall be with the condition that was placed upon Urdiñola, namely, that it shall not exceed the salary of the officials of Mexico.

Advantages of article 2.   To his Majesty it matters very little whether he has the power to name the first royal officials or whether the governor shall have authority to do it.   It is to be expected that married men of fortune, with children and families, will go on the expedition in confidence and that he [the governor] will have the means with which to reward them and honor them, and since they hold settled offices that they will remain permanently in the country, which is what most concerns his Majesty, and with this the kingdoms will be augmented and will not have the fears and burdens which, when they occur so near the beginnings, serve for nothing but to alarm [the people]. In this way each one will be in his own home, and after the country is won and pacified the way will be left open for his Majesty to name at his will the royal officials in case those named by the governor shall fail.

Disadvantages of modification 2. His Majesty has not at present any rents in those provinces, and therefore the Count makes the modification that the salaries of the officials shall not exceed those of Mexico. But he does not take notice that those provinces are 350 leagues further inland than Mexico, where the prices of things must be three times as high. If the land is richer it will be right that the salaries shall be greater, since they are to be paid from the fruits and products of it; if there are none they will not be paid, nor is there any reason for reducing them, especially for those who are to be the chief ones in the conquest and in winning the land for their king and natural lord.

3. Article. Item: That I and my said heirs and successors in the said government and jurisdiction must be and shall be under the immediate control of the royal Council of the Indies, so that none of the viceroys of this New Spain or of the neighboring audiencias shall have the power to interfere in the administration of the said government—as is provided in article 69 of the ordinances.

Ordinance 69. He and his son or heir or successor in the government and jurisdiction shall deal directly with the Council of the Indies, in such a manner that none of the viceroys or neighboring audiencias shall have the power to interfere in the administration of his province, either officially or on petition of a litigant or by writ of appeal, nor to provide commissioned judges. The Council of the Indies shall have the power to try the cases of the government officially or on petition of a litigant or by writ of appeal; in case of litigation between parties it shall try by writ of appeal civil cases of six thousand pesos up, and criminal cases in which the sentences impose pain of death or mutilation of members.

Modification. That the independence that he asks for of the viceroy and Audiencia of Mexico shall be renounced, and he shall formally consent to be subordinated to them respectively, to the viceroy in everything and for everything in all that has to do with war and finances, and to the Audiencia in what touches upon grievances of justice, this even to the amount that may seem right to it. Let his Majesty be consulted in regard to the exemption that is asked for, so that if it pleases him he may grant it.

Advantages of article 3. His Majesty grants in ordinance 69 that the governors shall be under the immediate control of the Council of the

Indies, and that in the pacified kingdoms and provinces this shall be practised so inviolably that no viceroy shall interfere in the administration of the governments, for every day occasions arise in which they have the power to do it and affairs in which it seems right [to them] that they should do so. The Count wishes that Don Juan shall be under the control of the viceroy in what concerns the war which he is carrying on at his own expense and danger, although he is so distant from him, especially in matters of war and conquests, whose execution does not admit delay in carrying out what it is necessary to do. And in what touches upon the *real hacienda,* as his Majesty has none at present [in that country] there is no occasion for disputing about it until it exists, and then his Majesty will give the order that is to be obeyed. And as to what concerns justice, the ordinance requires that it shall depend solely upon the royal Council of the Indies and be immediately subject to the governors, the more so as, since this kingdom is so distant from Mexico, and is so rich and full of people, it is clearly evident that in a very short time it will be placed under the jurisdiction of the Audiencia. The viceroy himself, perceiving that it is a very serious thing to modify this very important article, guarded himself by saying that his Majesty should be consulted in regard to the said exemption, so that if he pleased he could grant it.

Disadvantages of modification 3. One of the things that has done most to moderate the ardor of those who were moved to make this expedition is the little aid which the Count has given in conferring personal authority upon Don Juan, for, since he compelled Don Cristóbal, his brother, to renounce the right to be under the immediate control of the Council of the Indies, it seemed to everybody that for any occasion he would take it from him and send another in his place. For this reason many who were inclined to go did not get ready, for everything that the Count has done has been to diminish and cut down the powers and dignity of Don Juan, always addressing him as " you " in such letters as he wrote to him, very differently from what the viceroy Don Luís de Velasco, father of this viceroy Don Luís, did with Don Tristán de Arellano when he went to Florida, for he accompanied him from Mexico as far as the city of Tlaxcala, twenty leagues away, where, with the applause of all the soldiers, he took leave of him, calling him " your lordship ", whereby he dignified him as a personage and gave strength to the people and expedition. Both the one and the oher have been lacking in this, and it will become more evident every day if his Majesty does not encourage and favor what is now so discouraged, and always has been, by the Count of Monterey.

Article 4. Item: That I shall have the power to bring every year two ships for the provisioning of the country and for the exploiting of what mines there may be, free of import duties. Let it be granted to him in conformity with article 79 of the ordinances.

PETITION TO THE VICEROY BY DON JUAN DE OÑATE
FOR THE JOURNEY OF EXPLORATION AND
THE CAPITULATIONS OF THE VICEROY
September 21, 1595

Source: Charles Wilson Hackett, ed., Historical
Documents Relating to New Mexico, Nueva Viz-
caya, and Approaches Thereto to 1773, pp. 225,
227. Washington, D.C.: Carnegie Institution of
Washington, 1923. Courtesy of the Carnegie
Institution of Washington.

In the City of Mexico, on the twenty-first day of the month of September, 1595, before his Lordship, the viceroy, Don Luís de Velasco, this
petition was read. And, after he had examined what was asked for and
presented in it by Don Juan de Oñate, he said that in conformity with the
royal cédula directed to his lordship and dated at San Lorenzo on the
nineteenth of July of the past year of 1589, and the paragraph in a letter
of January 17, 1593, and another paragraph in another and last letter of
June 21, 1595—copies of which are to be placed with these memoranda—
he had accepted and did accept the offer of the person of the said Don
Juan de Oñate, and he had chosen him and did choose him for the exploration, pacification, and conquest of the provinces of New Mexico. And
responding in detail to the articles proposed by the said Don Juan, he
ordered that which is stated on the margin of each one. Don Luís de
Velasco. Before me MARTÍN LÓPEZ DE GAUNA.

Most Illustrious Sir: I, Don Juan de Oñate, resident of the city of
Nuestra Señora de las Zacatecas, of the new kingdom of Galicia, declare:
That, having offered to your most illustrious lordship my person to
serve his Majesty and your lordship in his royal name in the pacification
of New Mexico and the occasions that have offered, continuing in this
what I have done for more than twenty years up to now in the war with
and the pacification of the Chichimecas and Guachichiles Indians and
other nations in the kingdoms of Nueva Galicia and Vizcaya at my own
cost and expense, imitating my father, Cristóbal de Oñate, who, while
exercising the duty and office of captain-general in the said kingdom of
Galicia, conquered, pacified, and settled the major part of the said king-

dom at his expense. In this he spent a very large sum of money, as is known to your lordship and is public and notorious, following in the footsteps of his ancestors, who always employed themselves like noble knights in the service of the royal crown of Castile. And your lordship having been pleased to do me the favor of accepting my offer, and to order me to enter the said province in pursuit of Captain Francisco de Leyva Bonilla and his companions, so that they might be arrested and receive the punishment which their offense merited in having entered unlawfully and contrary to the order of your lordship and the special prohibition of his Majesty—not to mention the great difficulties that would result and will result from the disturbance and ill treatment of the natives, for cause of which their conversion and pacification will not be so easy in the future; and because the principal purpose that should be held and which his Majesty exhibits, and no less your lordship in his royal name, is this conversion, and the one is closely joined to the other; and because it would be possible to procure the punishment of the said delinquents and at the same time the service of God and the king, our lord, in the said conversion and pacification, I again offer to your lordship my person so that your lordship may thus be pleased to employ it in the said exploration, pacification, and conversion of the said provinces of New Mexico.

I beg that your most illustrious lordship will do me the favor to accept the said offer and to choose my person for the said purpose; and for what concerns it I present the following:

First, I offer to take two hundred men and over, equipped with everything necessary and supplies sufficient to reach the settlements and until after I have reached them—all at my expense and that of the said soldiers, without his Majesty being obliged to pay them any salary besides what I will voluntarily give them from my funds.

Item: 1500 pesos worth of flour and corn.
Item: 500 pesos worth of wheat for sowing.
Item: 500 pesos worth of jerked beef.
Item: 1000 head of cattle.
Item: 3000 sheep for wool.
Item: 1000 sheep for mutton.
Item: 1000 goats.

CONTRACT BETWEEN DON PEDRO PONCE DE LEÓN AND THE KING
FOR THE EXPLORATION OF NEW MEXICO
September 25, 1596

Source: Charles Wilson Hackett, ed., Historical
Documents Relating to New Mexico, Nueva Vizcaya, and Approaches Thereto to 1773, pp. 305,
307, 309. Washington, D.C.: Carnegie Institution of Washington, 1923. Courtesy of the Carnegie Institution of Washington.

*Contract and agreement with Don Pedro Ponce de León with regard to
the exploration, pacification, and settlement of New Mexico. [San
Lorenzo, September 25, 1596.]*

The King. Inasmuch as you, Don Pedro Ponce de León, whose residence is said to be in the town of Bailén, have informed me that, desiring
that our holy Catholic faith shall be exalted, proclaimed, and received in
more parts, and my crown, revenues, and patrimony increased, you
wished, with my approval, to explore, pacify, and settle the province of
New Mexico, of whose great size and wealth and extensive native population information has been received through religious and laymen who
have gone to that country at different times and occasions;

And inasmuch as you promise that you will endeavor, in the form that
I have given for making such explorations and in no other way, before
everything else to have our faith and gospel proclaimed, preached, and received, and after this is done to have the natives of the said province give
me voluntary obedience and recognition as their king and natural lord—
as I am, since the supreme lordship belongs to me in the said province
and in all the other provinces discovered or to be discovered in the West
Indies, because of the well-known grants and concessions which I have
enjoyed and do enjoy —without making use of the arms, soldiers, and
people with whom you enter the said province except to defend and
protect the ecclesiastical persons whom you have to take with you for
the proclamation of the holy gospel, or in your own defense, nor going
beyond what you ought to do in this in any manner or case;

And inasmuch as you voluntarily offer to pay all the expense that may be necessary for this service of God and myself from the rentals of your estate and patrimony, with expectation of the reward and favor which I shall grant you according to your character and service;

And inasmuch as the work and undertaking are so greatly to the service of God and myself, in consideration of all this I have decided that a contract and agreement shall be made with you in the following form:

1. First.   You, the said Don Pedro Ponce de León, agree to go to explore, pacify, and settle the said province of New Mexico at your own expense, without any obligation on my part to aid you in any manner from my funds, and in order to put it into execution [you promise] to sail within six months after I shall have signed this agreement.

2. Item: You agree to take with you six religious of the Company of Jesus, two to be given to you in these kingdoms and four in New Spain, as has already been arranged. By my order to their superiors and you it is understood that you are to give them at your expense the ornaments, chalices, bells, and everything else necessary for the celebration of divine worship.

3. Item: You agree that in the said New Spain you will raise and assemble three hundred soldiers, married and single, workmen to cultivate the land and herd cattle, and officials for all the offices. For this I give you permission to raise standards and establish treasuries in all the cities, villages, and towns of those kingdoms where it appears proper to you to take this measure, and you bind yourself to conduct these persons into the provinces of New Mexico well armed and mounted without obligation on my part to give them pay or any other recompense.

4. Item: You bind yourself to purchase flour and maize up to the sum of 22,000 reales to take with you.

5. 11,000 reales in wheat for sowing.

6. 6400 reales in jerked beef, 2000 head of cattle for breeding, and for the same purpose 5000 wool-bearing sheep and 3000 for mutton, 3000 goats, 400 heads of black cattle, 290   colts, and as many breeding mares.

7. Item: You agree to take six pairs of bellows with tools and implements for a forge.

8. Item: You agree to take also eight more pairs of bellows for mines.

9. Item: You agree to purchase iron for horseshoes with their nails to the amount of 22,000 reales to take with you.

10. Item: You agree to take 8000 reales worth of foot-gear.

11. Item: You agree to take as much as 12,000 reales worth of drugs or the cure of the sick.

12. Item: You agree to take as much as 10,800 reales worth of iron ools.

13. Item: You also agree to take as much as 2000 reales worth of articles for barter and gifts to the Indians.

14. Item: You also agree to take as much as 2600 reales worth of paper.

15. Item: And 12,000 reales in frieze and sackcloth.

16. Item: And to take thirty ox-carts provided with everything necessary.

17. All of the above you offer to take over and above the supplies and provisions for soldiers until they arrive at the settlements, for none of the above-mentioned is to be touched before then.

POWER GRANTED TO DON PEDRO PONCE DE LEÓN
AS GOVERNOR OF NEW MEXICO
October 16, 1596

Source: Charles Wilson Hackett, ed., Historical
Documents Relating to New Mexico, Nueva Vizcaya, and Approaches Thereto to 1773, p. 323.
Washington, D.C.: Carnegie Institution of Washington, 1923. Courtesy of the Carnegie Institution of Washington.

*Power granted to Don Pedro Ponce de León, who is going as governor
and captain-general to the provinces of New Mexico, to give Indians
in encomienda. [San Lorenzo, October 16, 1596.]*

Don Felipe, Q: Inasmuch as in the contract and agreement which I
ordered to be made with Don Pedro Ponce de León concerning the settlement and pacification of the province of New Mexico, there are two
articles by which I give him power to give in *encomienda* the divisions of
Indians that there may be in the said provinces among the pacifiers and
settlers of them, as is contained in the said articles as follows:—" Item,
you are granted. . . ." And because it is my will that what is contained
in them be kept and fulfilled, I give, by these presents, power and authority
to the said Don Pedro Ponce de León, in conformity with the said articles,
to give in *encomienda* all the divisions of Indians of the said provinces
in the best manner, bearing in mind that there shall be no excess in it,
but that each of those who may serve in the above shall receive in pro-
portion to his character and services, as may be seen that he deserves,
provided that the ports and capital cities shall be assigned to the crown,
and that he shall grant the *encomiendas* in accordance with the law of
succession, with the charges and conditions that have been ordered by me,
taking care that the ordinances, decrees, and measures that have been
given upon the food, treatment, and instruction of the Indians be kept,
and taxing them according to the New Laws and what has been ordered
concerning the tribute that they are to give to their *encomenderos,* so that
they shall pay that and nothing more, with the warning that those who
exceed in this shall be deprived of the said *encomiendas* and shall be dis-
qualified and incapacitated from holding those or any others. Given at
San Lorenzo, October 16, 1596. I THE KING. Countersigned by JUAN
DE YBARRA.

LETTER FROM DON JUAN DE OÑATE TO THE KING
March 15, 1598

Source: Charles Wilson Hackett, ed., Historical
Documents Relating to New Mexico, Nueva Vizcaya,
and Approaches Thereto to 1773, pp. 395, 397.
Washington, D.C.: Carnegie Institution of Washington, 1923. Courtesy of the Carnegie Institution of Washington.

*Letter from the governor and captain-general of New Mexico, Don Juan
de Oñate, to the king. [Río de las Conchas, March 15, 1598.]*

To our lord, the king, in his royal hands.
Sir: The difficulties that have been put in the way of the expedition to
the provinces of New Mexico, which is in my charge through a contract
made with me by Viceroy Don Luís de Velasco, have been so great that
it may be regarded as a miracle that it has been possible to adjust them.
I gave an account of the expedition to your Majesty, making a statement
of the damage caused me by the detention, and the losses which have followed from it, and how much it is costing me, and what I have suffered
for not giving up my resolution to make it in your service. Also [I gave
an account of] how, as though it were some wrongful act or might be
esteemed as mischievous, I met with contradictions and oppositions unworthy of Christian breasts, threatening that if the obedience which I so
punctiliously gave should fail in the smallest particular it would be sufficient to destroy all that had been done and put me in trouble. It is the
truth, although nothing was found upon which to base the injuries which
I have received, that they went on multiplying until, with the camp, I
started very slowly on February 7 of this year, taking eighty carts and
wagons loaded with the necessary stores and provisions, trusting that by
the compassionate assistance of God in my good intent I shall accomplish

the purpose of the expedition, to the increase of the holy Catholic faith and the advantage of your royal person. Dwelling little upon the great trouble which I have had in resisting the violent efforts of the Count of Monterey to dissuade me from going on, I do not know how to say that the project itself can be saved unless I go on, even though I believe that he has not ceased putting stumbling-blocks in my way.

On the fourteenth of the same month I sent Vicente de Zaldivar, *sargento mayor* of the camp, with sixteen men, to search out a new road from the Río de Conchas with a guide, who lost the road and direction. Notwithstanding this, he went on and arrived at the village of the Indians, by whom he was well received, although some, as many as fifty, of them took up arms and resisted him, without appreciating the kindness which he showed them, and compelled him to treat them with severity, after which they permitted him to pass from there. On the twenty-eighth of the same month he reached the river called El Norte, sixteen or twenty leagues from the first settlements of New Mexico. From there he returned, examining the road and judging it to be very good, with plenty of springs of water, well placed for its conservation, for sixty leagues from there to here. He heard of and avoided the village of the hostile Pataragueyes Indians, leaving it forty leagues to one side, on the right hand.

With this favorable beginning I am continuing the expedition and shall go on with it until its purpose is accomplished, and, until I die, I shall do my duty in serving your Majesty. Since at the beginning the door to it was closed and the viceroy was in opposition and I encountered nothing but obstacles, fearing this now, I shall be content if this letter and the duplicate of the one which I have already written to your Majesty reach your royal hands, without daring to send an explanation of the small credit that was given me by the one who took the muster from me the second time, with the desire of making me appear impecunious. I pray your Majesty, in the belief that my suffering deserves reward, to deign to order that the agreement made with me by Viceroy Don Luís de Velasco be kept, and that the favor that I deserve and that is due to one who has endured with patience, as I have, a flood of vexations, be granted me, with rewards in return for my labors, for I hope in God that the one I am now following will have great results. Of this I will give an account to your Majesty when I reach New Mexico, and I promise myself the reward for it from the hand of your Majesty, whose life may our Lord guard, with increase of great kingdoms in this part, as we, loyal subjects of your Majesty, desire. At the Río de las Conchas, March 15, 1598.

Don JUAN DE OÑATE.

GASPAR PÉREZ DE VILLAGRÁ'S ACCOUNT
OF THE EXPEDITION OF JUAN DE OÑATE
1598

Source: Gaspar Pérez de Villagrá, History of
New Mexico, trans. by Gilberto Espinosa, intro.
and notes by F.W. Hodge, pp. 41-45, 52, 59.
Los Angeles: The Quivira Society, 1933. Reprinted by Arno Press, Inc., 1967.

CANTO ONE

Which sets forth the purpose of this History, the location
of New Mexico, the news received concerning the
same; which also treats of the antiquity of the
Indians, and of the coming and descent
of the original Mexicans.

ARMS I sing, and of the deeds of that heroic son
who, despite the envy of men and unmindful of
the sea of difficulties which on every side beset
him, patiently, prudently, and bravely vanquished all and
performed most heroic deeds.

I sing the glory of those mighty Spaniards who in the
Western Indies, through many conflicts, penetrated and
discovered the most hidden portions of the earth. " Plus
ultra " is their cry as, with strong arm and mighty
courage, they carry on through conflicts as bitter as ever
recorded by unworthy pen.

Most Christian Philip, you are the Phoenix of New
Mexico, newly produced and come forth from those burning flames and embers of most holy faith, in whose glow-
ing coals we but recently saw your sainted father, our
sovereign, ablaze with holy zeal. Pray lay aside for the
time the cares and government of that mighty empire,
which in truth is supported only by your strong arm, and
listen, O, gracious prince, while I relate how that Christian Achilles of your choice, in your name, overcoming un-
believable obstacles, implanted the holy faith of Christ
among the heathen nations of New Mexico. If you will
but condescend to lend me your attention, who doubts but
that the entire world will pause and listen to a tale which
interests such a mighty prince.

Having secured your permission, I am yet mindful

that I have attempted to relate not only those deeds
worthy of recording, but also those I am most unworthy
to repeat. I pray that the spirits of those mighty heroes
of whom I sing will animate and give me courage and
speed my pen along its daring flight, that my words may
be worthy of their deeds.

Hearken, O, mighty king, for I was a witness of all
that I here relate!

Beneath the Arctic circle, at a latitude of thirty-three
degrees, which is the precise latitude of holy Jerusalem,
are found many remote and barbarous nations, far removed from the guidance of the holy church. Here the
longest day of the year is at its fourteenth hour when
the blazing sun has reached its summer solstice, from
which zenith it passes from Andromeda to Perseus. Such
a constellation always bears on Venus and Mercury.

In length this district extends, according to our best
knowledge of known meridians, two hundred and seventy
degrees in the temperate zone and fourth clime; two hundred leagues on the side bordering on the North sea and
the Mexican gulf. It approaches the coast more toward
the southeasterly winds and toward the rugged California and the Sea of Pearls. It is about an equal distance from the southwesterly winds. From the frozen
regions it is a good five hundred Spanish leagues. Within
this area are included some five thousand leagues. It is
pitiful to view this immense area and the many ignorant
people who inhabit these vast regions, all without knowledge of the blood of Christ or of His holy faith.

It is a well-known fact that the ancient Mexican races,
who in ages past founded the City of Mexico, came from
these regions. They gave the city their name that their
memory might be eternal and imperishable, imitating in
this the immortal Romulus who first raised the walls of
ancient Rome.

The above facts are established and verified by those
ancient paintings and hieroglyphics which these people
have and by means of which they carry on their barter
and communicate with one another, although not with
the ease and elegance with which we communicate with
absent friends by our excellent system of writing.

When once we had set forth upon our journey to
New Mexico, over uncertain and unknown paths, we
heard of wondrous things which corroborated these ancient legends. It was in the last settlements of what is
known as New Spain, and in the farthermost outposts of
the kingdom of Vizcaya. Here, having broken camp and
being ready to set forth into the unknown regions before
us, we were told of ancient traditions which had come
down from time immemorial, repeated from mouth to
mouth, much the same as the knowledge has come down
to us of those heroes who first came to Spain and conquered and colonized the land.

The natives of these regions, with one accord, repeated the same story. They said that from those
regions, pointing toward the north, where the north wind
hides, mid deep, boreal caverns, two most warlike
brothers came forth. These, descendants of kings and
sons of a mighty king, came, eager to win fame and glory
and seeking to conquer these countries and by force of
arms reduce the princes and rulers of these lands to such
an humble state that, like lambs to slaughter led, they
would willingly submit to the haughty power of their
mighty state.

Coming with a numerous and well-armed force, they
advanced in two mighty columns. The elder, with a great
number of his cohorts, led the advance, while the younger,
with an equal number of his warlike followers, closed the
rearguard. In the center came their immense baggage
train, their tents, and the brilliant banners which they

raised over their regal dwellings. Babes and children of
tender years, without number, played about their camp,
here and there, in childish fancy. In the midst of their
warlike quarters were seen, like beautiful flowers in the
midst of thorns, handsome matrons and lovely maidens,
bewitchingly and gorgeously arrayed, as did befit their
noble birth. Gallant and handsome youths, in the flower
of young manhood, all bedecked in holiday attire, vied
with one another in their nobleness and gallantry. They
would have done honor to the most gallant courtier in
the most exalted court.

In like manner, the heavy, well-formed squadrons, terrible in their fierce and numerous array, yet showed a
gay and noble appearance. Some sought to resemble the
fierce and noble lion, dressed in the skin of that most
royal beast; others covered themselves with the skins of
striped tigers, or with the habit of the gray and hungry
wolf; others appeared as hares, timid rabbits, great fish,
eagles, and every other animal; in fact, every form of life
that walks, swims, or flies was there, represented in most
natural form. This is a very ancient and original custom
which, we have found, prevails among all the peoples
and nations of the Indies that we have discovered.

Their arms were very efficient and warlike. They carried well-bent bows, with wide and strong quivers filled
with long, slender arrows; light darts; heavy war axes;
great war-clubs with heads studded with sharp bits of
obsidian; long, well-made slings; beautifully fashioned
and adorned shields, and numberless multi-colored banners and standards.

The long lines of well-trained footmen were divided
into groups, each of which bore its peculiar arms. As
they marched in gallant array, so great were their numbers that, despite the grassy meadows over which they
came, the sky was darkened by the cloud they raised,

and it seemed as though the very earth trembled under their feet.

As they marched with martial air, there suddenly appeared before their ranks a fierce demon in the shape of an old hag. So fierce and terrible were her features that before I can attempt to picture them, I must need pause awhile.

CANTO THREE

*How the Spaniards first discovered New Mexico; how
they made the first expeditions of discovery; who
went, and of others who planned the conquest.*

AN imperishable and noble symbol is the work of
the illustrious and memorable fame that we
cherish and treasure in the sovereign and
triumphant court and militant world in which we live;
this by virtue of the valiant heroes who upheld its immortal banner. Behold, worthy sir, the extent and height
of its fame is such that as an heroic and sublime shield
the all-powerful and eternal God chose to make man, in
His own image and likeness, that he might look up to
Him and honor Him.

If man wishes to be happy and free from care in this
life, he should accept with strong heart such trials as may
come to him, for even in these the greatness and goodness of God is manifest, showing clearly the beauty of
His noble deeds and actions. This is plainly shown to us,
as resplendent suns shining high above in the fourth
heaven, by the following.

While those courageous men, the negro Estévan,
Cabeza de Vaca, Castillo Maldonado, and Dorantes
were wandering through the wilds of Florida, in the
hours of their greatest trials and sufferings the Supreme
Being chose to protect them in many miraculous ways.
As God himself breathed life into men, and healed the
sick, the paralyzed, and the blind with the mere touch
of His palms, so these wanderers, as they journeyed
from tribe to tribe, not only cured the sick, the paralyzed,
and the blind, but also gave life to the dead with only
their blessing and holy breath, medicine which may be

found only in the miraculous apothecary of the powerful God.

The simple natives of these regions were astounded
and regarded these men as veritable gods. On one occasion they brought them as a tribute more than six hundred hearts of small animals they had killed.

It is to be wondered that people so ignorant and savage as these should realize that to beings who wrought
such deeds, sacrifice was due in deed as well as in heart.
Though their tribute was but a poor morsel to satisfy
the pangs of hunger, yet no one can overlook the nobleness of their spirit. The heart has no equal in the entire
body. In man it is the fundamental basis of all life; it
gives energy to his entire being. Everything which is
high and elevating, every urge the senses feel and regis-
ter, emanates from the heart. Nothing can destroy it
without first destroying the body in which it lives, for it
is the very last to perish. And in the heart, like in a
noble temple, dwells the soul in all its goodness. From
the heart the soul offers up to Almighty God its devout
and saintly prayers, its good works, its thoughts, its loves,
its tears and sighs. Being a gushing fountain from which
flow wondrous things, it should be offered up to God
alone and to those who follow in His holy steps.

We may take a lesson from these rude savages who
offered up so many hearts in sacrifice to those famous
five who wandered through their lands.

After wandering for nine long years, suffering in-
credible hardships, these five reached the province of
Culiacán, a land which in noble times past was settled
by most worthy men. Here a zealous Franciscan friar,
Marcos de Niza by name, having heard from the lips of
these travelers of the lands they had discovered, and
noting that their accounts corroborated what he had
heard from the natives of these regions, of those lands

to the north whence the original Mexicans came, determined to see these lands for himself. Like the great Columbus who gave a New World to Castile, imbued with the spirit of discovery, he prepared to set forth with a faithful companion to penetrate these regions for at least two hundred leagues. But the Supreme Being decreed otherwise. His companion fell ill, and so Niza, undaunted, set forth, accompanied only by a number of friendly Indians.

Marcos de Niza was not gone long. Like one who has discovered a precious treasure and hurriedly returns for aid, he came back quickly and gave word of the wonders he had seen and the cities he had discovered.

There is nothing in the world to compare with the presumptuousness of man. He attempts things which it seems are reserved for God alone. You will note, worthy king, that the great Cortés, Marquis of the Valley, who, after braving the dangers of the mighty deep, burned his fleet, determined either to conquer or to perish; this very one in whom the spirit of adventure still burned with an unconquerable desire to discover not one more world but one hundred if possible, having learned from the lips of [Fray Marcos de] Niza of those things which I have related, determined at once to conquer these countries and raise the cross of the true faith in these savage and benighted lands. Having determined upon the enterprise, he set his prow forward and with full sail began his plans.

Greed for power, like love, will permit no rival. Even as Caesar and Pompey clashed over their rival ambitions for world power, so now Cortés met with opposition. Disregarding the ancient friendship which existed between them, Don Antonio de Mendoza, the first viceroy of New Spain, thirsting for renown and glory, asserted that as viceroy it was his prerogative to lead the expedition. Heaven help us when personal ambitions and lust for power clash! Then neither king nor law, reason nor friendship, are considered. The Mantuan fittingly says: " O, damnable hunger for vain riches, what dire misfortunes you lead men into! " He gives them this holy, high, and exalted name so that no mortal will dare to seek them without justice. The Holy Scripture says, " Who can this person be, and, should we praise him because he performed such marvelous deeds during his lifetime? "

These two, as if they were powerful lords setting out to conquer the entire world, set to quarreling. Cortés claimed that as Adelantado of the South Seas the privilege should be his. Finally, better to accomplish his purpose, he set sail for Spain to lay his cause before your illustrious grandfather, Charles the Fifth, that wise and prudent king who so wisely governed the greatest empire of his day, being respected, loved, and honored by all mankind.

Having set sail for Spain, after a long and arduous journey, Cortés arrived home. Here like a powerful ship which has at last entered a safe port only to founder upon the rocks and sink, death met this mighty man saying, " I spare none," thereby putting an end to all his ambitions for this conquest. With a terrible certainty which admitted neither excuse nor delay, it ordered him upon that dreaded journey which we all must one day travel: that road which even those miserable souls who crave immortality must also know.

Like one who has let slip from his hands a precious vase and breathlessly sees it strike the ground and shatter in many pieces, so now the world stood aghast and speechless to see this noble son lying there still and cold, a miserable body, dust of the earth. He whose sword had been most powerful; he who had conquered an entire world, lay still in death. But who is powerful enough to resist this fate? Even popes and mighty kings are prostrated beneath its feet. All must obey its mandate. If the Son of God himself had to die, it is inevitable that all must finally go this way.

With this event Antonio de Mendoza, his rival now dead, was left unopposed upon the field, like one who has laid low his adversary in mortal combat. In order the better to carry out his plans, availing himself of that third divine gift,—reason, which guides us like a shining light, he took counsel with Cristóbal de Oñate, a man of good mind and keen judgment. Oñate was among the most renowned of those who ever drew sword in either New Spain or the kingdom of Peru.

Mendoza inquired of Oñate as to which of his men was the bravest, the most discreet, and the best fitted to lead an expedition in advance of the main army. Oñate did not pause to consider but, like the sagacious lynx or the daring eagle who acts on the instant, immediately replied by bringing before the viceroy his nephew Juan de Zaldívar, a worthy veteran tried in battle. To Zaldívar the viceroy gave the command of a gallant squadron of thirty picked Spanish lancers. With these Zaldívar set forth into the regions of the north, penetrating the country for a great distance, enduring sufferings and hardships which only their valor could have survived, as we shall see later.

In the meantime, the resourceful Mendocino [Mendoza] assembled a large and well-equipped army of gallant troops who vied with one another in their martial air and finery. Seeing such a great army assembling, [Fray Marcos de] Niza, the provincial of the Franciscans, joined them, rejoicing at this opportunity to carry the Gospel to these poor heathen peoples.

Since no body can function without a head, Francisco

Vázquez Coronado, a man of merit and worth, was chosen leader. He was given the rank of general in recognition of his ability. The viceroy, in order to show him honor and to encourage the troops, accompanied him in person as far as Compostela, some two hundred leagues from the City of Mexico.

Captain Zaldívar and his command, fighting their way and suffering greatly from hunger and thirst, penetrated far into the regions ahead and, returning, met the army at Compostela. Here he informed the viceroy that the country he had discovered seemed of but little value. He said that it was poor and desolate, and the natives destitute and savage. He urged caution that this news should not be spread about lest it be the occasion for a retreat. For, he reasoned, even where others have lost hope, the skilful hunter who joyfully pursues the chase often is rewarded with a heavy catch. There are, however, always some who oppose every enterprise of merit. There were not lacking those who talked and stirred up opposition, saying it would be a misfortune indeed that the army should waste its efforts in such a poor enterprise.

The viceroy was bitterly disappointed at these reports but, considering the same, prudently hid his feelings as best he could. Realizing that the situation was critical, he ordered that not a word be said of these reports. He well knew that should these rumors be noised about, the entire expedition would be abandoned. The expense of the expedition had already been incurred. Cristóbal de Oñate alone had generously given fifty thousand pesos in gold for the enterprise. The viceroy reasoned, moreover, that a second entry into the country might prove more profitable than the first. So, he gave his orders for the newly appointed general to proceed and, having bade the army farewell, he returned to Mexico.

With great difficulty the army marched as far as the
pueblo of Cíbola and other nearby towns. These were
the same towns which had been visited by Zaldívar, by
the Floridans [Cabeza de Vaca and his companions],
and by [Fray Marcos de] Niza. The general was over-
joyed at seeing these towns and declared a holiday. He
himself went ahead, mounted on a fiery steed. In a
skirmish he was unhorsed and fell to the ground with
such force that he was rendered senseless.

Just as when the head suffers the entire body is in
pain, so the soldiers, lacking a leader and seeing their
general helpless and grievously wounded, began to com-
plain and murmur of the hardships they endured. They
complained bitterly of the great cities they were told of
but never saw and despairingly clamored to be led back
to their homes. It would have been far better had they
never undertaken this expedition than to have so dis-
gracefully abandoned it.

Finally, the murmuring and dissatisfaction reached
such a point that it was determined to turn back. This
was not without many a firm and bitter remonstrance
from many brave and valiant men who sought to dissuade and reason with the soldiers. Among these were
the saintly [Fray Marcos de]Niza, the brave Don Francisco de Peralta, the bold veteran Zaldívar, and also that
distinguished warrior, Pedro de Tovar, the father of
Doña Isabel, a lady of most surpassing beauty, highest
virtues, and most estimable qualities, all inherited from
her illustrious father. He and many others unsuccessfully
insisted that the expedition continue.

The dissatisfaction was too great. The common rab-
ble, as might be expected, would not listen to arguments
or reason and only thought of their own desires. Their
insistence and stubbornness were such that all was
abandoned. Because they did not stumble over bars of

gold and silver immediately upon commencing their march into these regions, and because the streams and lakes and springs they met flowed crystalline waters instead of liquid golden victuals, they cursed the barren land and cried out bitterly against those who had led them into such a wilderness. Complaining and bewailing their fate, more like women than men, they left all behind and turned their backs upon the expedition they had begun. It is well to pause here rather than to continue the details of such a shameful tale.

TITLE OF ADELANTADO OF THE PROVINCES OF NEW MEXICO
FOR DON JUAN DE OÑATE
February 7, 1602

Source: Charles Wilson Hackett, ed., Historical
Documents Relating to New Mexico, Nueva Vizcaya,
and Approaches Thereto to 1773, pp. 397, 399, 401.
Washington, D.C.: Carnegie Institution of Washing-
ton, 1923. Courtesy of the Carnegie Institution of
Washington.

Don Juan de Oñate. Title of adelantado of the provinces of New Mexico
for Don Juan de Oñate, governor and captain-general of them.
[Villalpando, February 7, 1602.]

Don Felipe . . . Inasmuch as upon your part, Don Juan de Oñate,
governor and captain-general of the province of New Mexico, which is in
New Spain, the statement has been made to me that by one of the articles
of the contract which was made with you by my orders in regard to the
exploration, pacification, and settlement of the said provinces, Don Luís
de Velasco being my viceroy of New Spain, it was promised you that you
would be given the title of governor of the said provinces for your life
and for that of a son or heir, to which you should be appointed, in con-
cormity with the contents of an article of the instructions for new discoveries and settlements of the Indies,
And, inasmuch as supplication has been made to me upon your part
that, in view of the expenses which you have incurred in the journey and
the troubles which you have endured, I should order that it be approved,
I have decided favorably upon it, after being advised so to do, and by
these presents it is my will and pleasure that now and henceforth, for all
the days of your life you shall be my governor of the said provinces of
New Mexico and of the towns that may be settled in them, and after you
your son or heir or any person whom you may name. As such you shall
have the power to exercise the said office in all affairs pertaining and
belonging to it, according and as it is exercised by my governors of my
kingdoms of Castile and of the said Indies.
In the use and exercise of the said office and the practice of the rights

pertaining to it, you shall observe, and you and your said son or heir or person whom you may name shall be under obligation to observe, the laws and decrees of these my kingdoms which regulate it. You shall be empowered to enjoy and you shall enjoy and there shall be secured to you all the honors, grants, favors, franchises, privileges and exemptions, preferences, prerogatives, immunities, and all and every one of the other things which by reason of being my governor you have the right to have and enjoy and that ought to be secured to you. You shall have and receive the salary, rights, and other things owing and pertaining to the said office of governor, and, by this, my letter, I command my councillors, justices, *regidores,* gentlemen, squires, officials, and all good men of all the cities, towns, and villages of the said province of New Mexico, that they shall receive and hold you and your son or heir or person whom you may name as my governor; that they shall exercise the said office with you and with him in all the cases and affairs pertaining and belonging to it, and shall observe and cause to be observed all the honors, grants, favors, franchises, privileges, exemptions, preferences, prerogatives, immunities, and all and every one of the other things that by reason of the said office you have the right to have and enjoy and that ought to be secured to you; and that they shall pay and cause to be paid before everything the rights and salaries due and pertaining to it, in full and complete, with no decrease to you in anything, in accordance with the method which has been practised and in which payments have been made, and as they ought to be practised and made, with the other governors who have been and are in these my kingdoms of Castile and in the Indies. They shall not place or allow to be placed any obstacle or impediment against you in it or any part of it; for I by this writing receive and have received you into the use and exercise of it, and I give you the power and authority to make use of it [this writing] in case that you shall not be received in it [the office] by them or any one of them. Given at Villalpando, February 7, 1602. I THE KING. I, JUAN DE YBARRA, secretary to our lord the king, by whose order it was written. The licentiate LAGUNA, Doctor ANTONIO GONZÁLEZ, the licentiate PEDRO BRAVO DE SOTO MAYOR, Doctor EUGENIO DE SALAZAR, the licentiate VILLAGUTIERRE CHUMACEN.

THE COUNCIL OF THE INDIES TO THE PRESIDENT
OF THE CASA DE CONTRATACIÓN
June 12, 1602

Source: Charles Wilson Hackett, ed., Historical
Documents Relating to New Mexico, Nueva Vizcaya,
and Approaches Thereto to 1773, p. 401. Washington, D.C.: Carnegie Institution of Washington,
1923. Courtesy of the Carnegie Institution of Washington.

The *maestre de campo* of the expedition to New Mexico, Vicente de
Zaldívar, whom Don Juan de Oñate, in whose charge this exploration is,
sent to these kingdoms on business of that expedition, has represented
that it is necessary for the prosecution of the undertaking that there be
sent from these kingdoms some musketeers, and professional ship-
builders   in order to construct vessels and discover a port in those seas,
for there is a lack of such people in that country. Also he has petitioned
that he be given permission to raise and recruit in Seville and San Lucar
as many as sixty persons of this class, and that embarkation be given him
on his Majesty's account. His Majesty, having taken advice with regard
to it, has decided to grant him permission to collect, recruit, and take in
the fleet as many as forty men of this profession, and that your grace and
the official judges shall arrange with the masters of the merchant ships
of the said fleet for the supplies and provisions for them until they disem-
bark at San Juan de Ullua. Whatever this amounts to—provided that
the aid which his Majesty is giving to Don Juan de Oñate, for this purpose, for this time only, does not come to more than 1500 ducats—shall
be paid in New Spain from the funds of his Majesty in one of the royal
treasuries of Vera Cruz or Mexico. His Majesty has also ordered that
your grace and the official judges shall seek two pilots, experienced and
expert, who are required for the mapping of the routes to be traversed
in that expedition, and arrange with them to make this voyage, letting
them make it at the expense of the said Don Juan de Oñate; this you shall
do and arrange for everything, as is proper. And inasmuch as it is the
pleasure of his Majesty to grant to his grace permission that they may
take on the said journey the arms mentioned in the list that goes with

this, you will allow the said *maestre de campo* to take them, after examining them carefully and making a record of them. For the Marquis of Montesclaros you will give a list of those which they carry on board and take with them, so that by it in New Spain he can inspect and distribute them to the best advantage for the said expedition and see that they are not converted into other merchandise. To the preparation and despatch of all this you will give much haste, because of the early departure of the fleet and the necessity that the *maestre de campo* shall go in it. In conformity with this the said despatch has been sent to be signed by his Majesty, and in order to save time the Council has resolved to inform you by this writing of the decision which his Majesty has made in this matter. Valladolid, June 12, 1602. Signed by the Council.

PLAN FOR THE ERECTION OF A GOVERNMENT AND GENERAL
COMMANDANCY IN THE PENINSULA OF CALIFORNIA AND
THE PROVINCES OF SINALOA, SONORA, AND NUEVA VISCAYA
1768

Source: Irving Berdine Richman, California
Under Spain & Mexico 1535-1847, pp. 503-13.
New York: Houghton Mifflin Co., 1911.

IF, since the glorious Conquest which the great Hernan
Cortes made of the broad Domains which come under the name
of Nueva España, effort had been made by his Successors in this
Government to Second and to carry out the lofty designs of that
Hero, the Light of the Gospel and the supremacy of the August
Kings of España would have reached even to the utmost Bounds,
not yet known, of this immense Continent. But as the spirit of
activity and of Conquest was extinguished with the life of that
inimitable Man, with his death came to an end the rapid ad-
vances which he accomplished in this new World; and at last
we have not even maintained and conserved the possession
which we enjoyed, in undisturbed tranquillity, of the richest
territories on the Frontiers of Sonora and Nueva Viscaya.

The more immediate (and perhaps the exact) causes of this
failure, and of the veritable ruin which has befallen the unfortunate inhabitants of those Provinces, with grave injury to the
State, are, in reality, the utter neglect with which they have
been regarded at Mexico in these latter years; the considerable
distance at which they are situated, more than Six Hundred
Leagues, from this Capital; and the pressing Crowd of more
immediate business and cares which engross the entire attention
of any Viceroy of Nueva España. For, as he is not supplied with

Subordinates to assist him, it is not possible for him to make active provision, or for the influence of his authority to be felt, at the remote confines of an almost boundless Empire.

This practical knowledge which the present Viceroy has been acquiring, with no less discomfort than hardship, and the favorable opportunity afforded to him by the present expedition to Sonora, have made him reflect very seriously on the means which may be most suitable and efficacious for reëstablishing this great Monarchy in its earlier prosperity, and to put the distant Provinces into condition for maintaining themselves with Vigor, and for enlarging the [Spanish] domination — extending at the same time the Catholic Faith, in acknowledgment and reward for which God is allotting to the Crown of España the Richest Empires of the Universe.

With the view, then, of establishing in the uncultivated Provinces of this [new] world good order and Justice, and the opulence which is natural for them if they are placed under proper management, he proposes, and sends to the Viceroy by this post, another and separate Plan for Intendancies, in imitation of those which exist in the Metropolitan Province. And to the end that Our Sovereign the King may secure the important advantages of quickly aggrandizing the Rich Frontiers of this Empire, he has come to an agreement with the Visitador-General to develop the idea of a General Commandancy, suitably empowered, which shall comprehend under its exclusive administration the aforesaid Provinces of Sonora, Sinaloa, Nueva Viscaya, and the Peninsula of Californias. That region will now begin to recognize the Spanish Power, and to repay part of the great amount that it has cost the Crown and the Nation since its discovery and the foundation of the first Jesuit Missions.

What has most contributed to this idea — which the Viceroy and the Visitador regard as very serviceable, and its execution as quite indispensable — is the previously planned decision which has been reached in Council, and fully approved, that the Visitador shall go to establish Settlements in the said Provinces, and organize the Government of the latter with full powers and Commission from the Viceroy. The object of this action is to facilitate and hasten the erection of such Government and Commandancy upon the footing which is proposed in this Plan, since obstacles can never arise between two faithful Servants of the King who, Moving toward the same end, with upright intentions, always agree in their discussions and unite their efforts, with mutual concessions.

In view of these facts, and with the further incentive of having seen a project which was laid before the Lords Ministers of Madrid in December, 1760, for the creation of a Viceroyalty independent from that of Mexico, and including all the Provinces situated in the great district under the jurisdiction of the Audiencia of Guadalaxara, the Viceroy and the Visitador have concluded that it will be much more advantageous and less expensive to establish an authorized Government and General Commandancy in the three frontier Provinces. For [such a Government], possessing all the powers necessary to maintain them free from the invasions of the Barbarians, and gradually to extend their boundaries, will render them of use to their Sovereign Master; and it will be responsible only to the Chief who represents him in these Domains, and subordinate to him only so far as to report Affairs to him and to request his aid when that may be necessary.

In this manner will be avoided the difficulties, always odious, which usually arise over jurisdiction or limits between coördinate officials when they have similar duties; and by surrendering to the Commandancy of the Frontier Provinces the entire authority — which is indispensable in regions so far distant, in order not to cause failure in opportunities and in the most important projects — the exceedingly important object will be attained of furnishing life and movement to regions so extensive, fruitful and rich by Nature, which can in a few years form a New Empire, equal or even superior to this one of Mexico.

Nor are these advantages and utilities, although great, the only ones which the proposed new Government will yield; for as soon as the activity of a Commandant with authority and energy is felt, many dangers can be averted which now threaten us, by way of the South Sea, from certain foreign Powers who now have an opportunity and the most eager desire to establish some Colony at the Port of Monterrey, or at some other of the many harbors which have already been discovered on the western Coasts of this new World.

In this report is purposely omitted extended discussion of the continual attempts by which France and England have striven, for some two centuries, to find a passage from the Northern to the Southern Sea — especially by their Colonies in this North America — and of the exertions that the Russians are making, through the Sea of Tartary, to penetrate into our Indias. This is partly because Field-Marshal Don Antonio Ricardos departed from here the year before, with the purpose of presenting an elaborate Memorial on these facts, which are more easy to verify in Europe; and partly because the Prime Minister of España knows very well that the English — who now, as a result of the last War, are Masters of Canada and a great part of Luciana [Louisiana] — will spare no expense, diligence, or hardship to push forward the discoveries which the French made through those Colonies, a new Viceroyalty. It has seemed proper to put forth this idea clearly, for the reasons above explained, as well as to avoid so great expenses, when the same results can be obtained by means of the Commandancy which is proposed in this Plan.

Nor is it reckoned expedient that the new Governor and Commander-in-Chief establish his residence in the City of Durango, the Capital of Nueva Viscaya, as was proposed in the year 1760 — not only because that Town is very distant from Sonora, and much farther from the Californias, which at the present time need an active and continual promotion; but because (from the necessity of stationing an Intendant in Durango, if the Separate Plan which is sent be approved), the establishment which is therein proposed would be in any event less advantageous [at Durango]. For the Governors who have hitherto administered Nueva Viscaya have all (excepting the present one) lived in the Town of San Felipe de Chihuahua, which is the Frontier settlement and a very important Mining Centre, where the presence of a Governor who can defend it is certainly needed.

In this connection, likewise, [it may be noted] that for the present the Audiencia of Guadalaxara remains in that Capital, where it was established, with the object of avoiding the great expenses which would assuredly be caused by its transfer; and if in the course of time (which must make known the benefits that the General Commandancy will produce) it shall seem expedient, as it may, to locate the Superior Tribunal of Nueva Galicia, or to erect another, in the Capital which is to be established in Sonora, it would be very easy to carry out that plan then at little expense, and with the knowledge which experience furnishes in all human affairs.

What is judged to be certainly indispensable, and to be immediately effected, is the erection of a central Settlement on the confines of Sonora — either on the shore of the Gila River, or very near it (arrangements being meanwhile made to set up the Government at the Mission of Caborca, as being the station most advanced toward the Frontier), or else at the junction of that River and the Colorado. Then, the Capital of the New Government being located at almost equal distances from the Californias and Nueva Viscaya, its Chief with his administrative measures can proceed to either Province with the same ease

and indeed he ought to travel through them and visit all places, in order that by examining them with his own eyes, and gaining specific knowledge from being actually in the field, he may be enabled to shape his course with good judgment.

No less necessary and useful will be a Mint, which ought to be erected in that same Capital of Sonora, in order that Commerce may have free course, to the benefit of the public and of the Royal Treasury; and that the poor Vassals who have settled in those remote regions may not be under the painful necessity of transporting all the Gold and Silver to Mexico. [This they have done], with only damages and great expenses which utterly ruin them, or, when not so heavy, deprive them of the profits which the richness of the Ores would allow them if they could sell those metals in the same Region where they dig and Smelt them. And, lest it be feared that the establishment of a Mint in that Province would cause notable diminution in the Output of the Mint at Mexico, that of Sonora could be restricted to the coining of only a Million *pesos* each year; for that sum would be sufficient at present to supply that province with Money and to give a like share to the Californias and Nueva Viscaya — where, in truth, through the lack of Money, the King is suffering a great diminution in his Imposts, and the inhabitants intolerable grievances.

In the Capital which should be founded, a Bishop's See also ought to be erected, setting aside for the support of this New Dignity the Province of Sonora, also Sinaloa (which belongs to the Bishopric of Durango, and is at the considerable distance of more than Two Hundred and Fifty leagues), and the Peninsula of Californias. Although the last-named, as is claimed, is included in the Diocese of Guadalaxara, neither the reverend Bishops nor their Visitadors ever possessed any acquaintance with it; and consequently neither is the See of Nueva Galicia injured by the separation of Californias, nor is the loss which that of Durango will actually experience by cutting off from it Sonora and Sinaloa worthy of consideration, for in those territories there are very few Curates and the tithes are almost nothing. But these will very soon be increased, with the Government and General Commandancy in the undeveloped territories which are assigned to the new Bishopric.

It would be idle to enumerate the great [advantages] which the Bishop's See that is proposed in the Metropolis of Sonora would confer on Religion and the state; for the ardent zeal and Apostolic ministry of a Diocesan Prelate would immensely advance the conversion of the Heathen, hastening their reduction by influences near at hand, and conquering many souls for the Creator, at the same pace with which new Domains are acquired for the Sovereign who is His Immediate Vicar in the world. And it is certain that in no part of America are there so fine opportunities and so abundant a harvest as in the confines of Sonora and in the Missions of Californias; for the Tribes of Indians are exceedingly numerous, and their natural disposition renders them most easily persuaded of the infallible truth of the Catholic faith.

In view of these just considerations, the erection of the new
See should not be considered a burden, even though it might
be necessary at the beginning to assist the Prelate and his
limited Church with some revenue from the Royal Treasury;
for such pension would not continue long, when we consider
the natural fertility of those lands — which, placed under cultivation, will yield the most abundant produce — and just as
certainly would the Royal Estate be repaid [for this outlay]
and even much more, on account of the richness of the Mines
in those Provinces, which are well understood and known by
all.

As to what is proper for the General Commandant, it is proposed that he should be independent of the Audiencia and President of Guadalaxara; and it would be necessary to confer on
him the salary of twenty thousand *pesos*, in order that he may
have barely means on which to live with any [suitable] display
in those remote regions, and to meet the expenses of his journeys
from one Province to another, without its being necessary for
him to avail himself of the [extra] imposts, [now] condemned,
which have been tolerated in the Indias, and which have brought
them into the melancholy decadence which they are suffering
up to the present time. If perchance this salary, and those of
the three Intendants who in another Plan are proposed by the
Californias, Sonora, and Durango, shall seem excessive, it will be
easy to make it evident by experience that the Treasury will
be well indemnified for the amount of all these expenses. For
after the second year from the establishment of these positions
the amount allotted to them certainly cannot reach even the
tenth part of the increase which will appear in one branch of revenue alone, the fifths of the Silver and the Gold which may be
dug and smelted in Sonora and Californias. To this must be
added the revenue from the Pearls; from that fishery, although
it might be very abundant on the Coasts of that Peninsula,
nothing has been thus far produced to the Royal Treasury.

The greatest saving of expense which should be reckoned upon
to the benefit of His Majesty is in the very large expense-
accounts [*situados*] of the many Garrisons [*Presidios*] which exist

in the Californias, Sonora, and Nueva Viscaya; for, as the profitable idea of establishing Settlements on the Frontiers of these Provinces has for its aim to guard them from the invasions of the Infidel Indians, it will result in liberation from the useless and insupportable burden of so many Garrisons, which, as events prove, are of little or no use. For, although six of these are maintained in the Province of Sonora alone, it is more often invaded and more devastated, than the others — because those Garrisons are, in effect, really Rancherías, and chiefly serve to enrich the Captains and their outfitters.

It is true that, in order to garrison the Capital that is projected in Sonora and to guard the chain of Settlements on the Frontiers (which should be quasi-Military), two Companies of Dragoons and three of Mountain Fusileers, each of a hundred men, will be needed; but nothing is easier than to fill out this force by adding fifty recruits to the two [companies?] who have gone on the Sonora expedition. Taking for granted that the expense of these Veteran Bodies hardly reaches the third part of that which is caused at present by the Garrisons, it is clear that the Royal Treasury, thus coming out with much profit, would be able to pay the salaries of the Commandancy and intendancies; and the Frontiers of the three Provinces would be really shielded from the incursions of the Barbarians. For the new Towns, protected by the Squads into which the Fusileer Companies should be divided, could immediately be put into condition to defend their respective territories, and in time to aid in extending the [Spanish] domination — in view of which, and with these obligations, the Colonists must be established in the new Settlements, giving to each one the Arms necessary for his defense.

With the five Companies of Veteran Infantry and Cavalry, the Militia which the new Towns ought to form, and those who may be recruited in the Town of San Felipe de Chihuahua and its vicinity, it is estimated that the new General Commandant will be able for the present to maintain the defense of the Provinces embraced in his Government. If afterward he shall need, as is probable, larger forces for the expeditions which he

will find expedient to send out for the purpose of advancing the
Conversions and discoveries, it should not be difficult to increase
the troops, either regular or provincial, when experience makes
known the great benefits which are promised by this useful establishment in Provinces which are undoubtedly more abundant
and rich in mineral products than any others that have been
discovered in this Northern America.

Recently news has come that [the English have gone] as far
as the Lake of Bois, from which issues the deep-flowing River
of the West, directing its course, as discovered, toward the
Sea of that name; and if it empties therein, or reaches the South
Sea, or is (as may be the case) the famous Colorado River, which
forms the Gulf of Californias, there is no doubt, in whichever of
these alternatives, that we already have the English very near
to our Settlements in New Mexico, and not very distant from
the Western Coast of this Continent of America.

Moreover, the Prime Minister of our Court knows, from the
voyages and memoirs that are published in Europe, that the
Russians have been gaining an intimate knowledge of the
navigation of the Sea of Tartary; and that they are, according
to very credible and well-grounded statements, carrying on
the Fur Trade on a Continent or Island which, it is estimated,
lies at the distance of only eight hundred leagues from the
Western Coast of Californias, which runs as far as Capes Mendocino and Blanco.

But, while the attempts of Russia and England need not
revive at this time all the suspicions and anxieties that Spain
manifested in former days (especially after the Reign of Felipe
Second) for discovering and gaining possession, by way of the
South Sea, of the alleged passage which the other Nations were
seeking by way of the North Sea, it is indubitable that since the
year 1749 [sic] — in which Admiral Anson came to the Western
Coast of this Kingdom, as far as the entrance to the Port of
Acapulco — the English and the Dutch (who afterward brought
their ships from Eastern India within sight of Cape San Lucas
and the Coasts of New Galicia) have acquired a very detailed
knowledge of the Ports and Bays which we hold on the South

Coast, especially in the Peninsula of Californias. With all this no one can regard it as impossible or even very difficult for one of those two Nations or for the Moscovites to establish, when that is least expected, a Colony at the Port of Monterrey, where they would have all desirable facilities and conveniences; and that thus we should come to see our North America invaded and exploited by way of the South Sea as it has been by that of the North.

In these circumstances, it seems as if worldly prudence may counsel, and even carry into effect, that we should take proper precautions in time, putting into practice whatever measures may be feasible to avert the dangers that threaten us. And, as at present the Peninsula of Californias is free from obstruction, it follows that we should and easily could — its population being increased by the aid of the free Commerce which ought to be carried on between that territory and this Kingdom — transport a Colony to the Port of Monterrey with the same vessels that we now have in the South Sea, which have been built for the use of the Sonora expedition. It only remains to establish in this Province the General Commandancy, which very soon can promote and facilitate the Settlement of Monterrey, and of other points on the Western Coast of the same Californias — where there are good Harbors, and the soil is more fertile and productive than that of the North Shore.

A Chief who is on the ground and energetic will secure considerable extensions to the Frontiers of Sonora and Nueva Viscaya, unless he is insufficiently provided with the funds that are necessary in order that the establishment of his Government may produce the utilities and advantages that ought to be expected. These are set forth at length in the project, already cited, which was presented to the Court in the year 1760, with the aim of securing the erection [of such a Government]. If the decision be reached that it is more expedient to maintain on the Frontiers of Chihuahua an Official, subordinate to the Governor, for the defense of that Mining Centre, a suitable person for that employ. is Captain Don Lope de Cuellar, who was appointed by the Viceroy in fulfillment of the instructions addressed to him for the expulsion of the regulars belonging to the Company [of Jesus]. As that measure would do away with the office of *corregidor* that was established in that Town, which enjoys very considerable imposts, from the fund that they produce can be drawn the Salary of two thousand *pesos*, which of course will be an addition to his pay sufficient to maintain the said Governor. At the same time he ought to look after the affairs of the Royal Treasury, with rank as Deputy of the Intendant of Nueva Viscaya — who must reside in the Capital City of Durango, and be, like the Intendants of Sonora and Californias, directly subordinate to the General Commandant of the three Provinces, since that Chief is responsible for rendering account to the Viceroy of Nueva España of whatever enterprises he may undertake, and of all occurrences worthy of note in the region under his command.

An examination of this plan will make evident at first view that in it are discussed only the principal points and designs of the idea, and that its sole aim, with nothing else in view, is to promote the public Interests of the King and the State in an establishment which, besides the urgent necessity of effecting it, carries the special recommendation that it will be very advantageous in a short time; for, from now on, the Foundations of the Work are going to be laid with Solidity, Integrity, and Zeal.

At Mexico, the twenty-third of January, [in the year] One Thousand, Seven Hundred, and Sixty-Eight.

DON JOSÉ DE GÁLVEZ.

To the Marqués de Croix.

FATHER JUNÍPERO SERRA REPORTS ON CALIFORNIA MISSIONS
1773

In a report dated March 13, 1773, the indefatig-
able missionary Junípero Serra reported to Viceroy Antonio de Bucareli on the success of his
missionary activities.

Source: Antoine Tibesar, ed., Writings of Junípero
Serra, pp. 295-327. Washington, D.C.: Academy
of American Franciscan Sciences, 1955. Copyright 1955 by the Academy of American Franciscan Sciences.

It is of the utmost importance that the missions be provided with
laborers, to till the land, and so raise the crops for their maintenance
and progress. We would already have made a start in so doing,
were it not for the opposition of the Officer at the presidio—a situation I have described recently in a letter to the Reverend Father
Guardian of our College, written about the middle of October, from
San Diego. The original of that letter was turned over to the government offices of Your Excellency, where you may see it.

The easiest method seems to me the one we have presented from
the beginning. I explained it in the said letter. It is this. Along
with the sailors aboard ship, there should be a number of young
men from the vicinity of San Blas. I should think that it would not
be hard to find among them day laborers, cowboys and mule
drivers. These should be divided among the missions—six to each,
or four at least. But a rule should be made that the Officer of the
presidio has no right to change them for a whole year; and that
stipulation will inspire confidence in their minds. Otherwise, not a
single one will be found to be willing to stay, especially as matters
go now. Also, during the year their pay should be on the same basis
as that of the sailors at San Blas; and in the missions they should
receive free rations. And if at the end of the first year they wish
to stay a second year, the same treatment should be continued. If
they prefer to return to San Blas, by boat, they should be granted
their request, and others should be provided to take their place.

It is of no less importance that, when the livestock arrives, which

Your Excellency, in virtue of your decree, orders to be forwarded
from California for the equipment of the Monterey missions, some
Indian families from the said California should come, of their
own free will, with the expedition, and that they should receive
every consideration from the officials. They should be distributed, at
least two or three being placed in each mission. By taking such
measures two purposes will be accomplished. The first will be that
there will be an additional two or three Indians for work. The
second, and the one I have most in mind, is that the Indians may
realize that, till now, they have been much mistaken when they
saw all men, and no women, among us; that there are marriages,
also, among Christians. Last year, when one of the San Diego
Fathers went to California to get provisions, which had run short in
that mission, he brought back with him, along with the rest of his
company, two of the said families. At his arrival, there was quite a
commotion among the new Christians, and even among the gentiles;
they did not know what to make of these families, so great was
their delight. Just to see these families was a lesson as useful to
them as was their happiness at their arrival. So if families other
than Indian come from there, it will serve the same purpose very
well—that is, if we can provide for them. . . .

As regards our food supply—to last us a year, and to leave something over to give, at least, to the little Christian boys and girls—
I intended to say a great deal, but will limit myself to this: that our
sufferings are great; never have we, the religious, been in such dire
straits, and never has the said Officer been living in such plenty,
as since the time he and we arrived in Monterey. May our poverty
be accepted for the love of God, and may his plenty—I do not envy
him it—do him good. What I do want and ask for is, that the
missions be maintained, that there should be a mouthful over and
above to give to our Christians and catechumens, and that Chris-
tianity be extended.

Only two Indians from California still remain at my San Carlos
Mission. The rest I distributed among the other missions. When the
Officer was partitioning out what was brought by pack train, and
marked for Monterey, I asked him to make an entry in his accounts
for the two said Indians, to which he replied that he would not give
anything to any Indian, and that if I wanted to chase them away,
I should do so.

To sum up the whole situation, my opnion is that, without a
doubt, whatever, in your goodness, Your Excellency, or the King—
whom God keep—sends us—and without it at the present time we

could not keep going, nor could the missions be kept in existence —should be sent from here marked and addressed separately. I have already mentioned in the letter referred to, that this year the Missions of San Diego and San Gabriel are in poorer condition than last year, even though two boats arrived, while there was only one the year before. The explanation is that last year there was sent from here the full quota of supplies for San Diego, on the supposition that the packet boat *San José* had never reached there. And, in point of fact, it never did arrive. . . .

In view of what I have just told you, I earnestly ask Your Excellency for an additional forge and blacksmith. If it were set up at the Carmel Mission it could also serve the Missions of San Antonio and San Luis. Not only would we get better service, but we would be able to have some of the newly converted youths learn the trade. This the Fathers of said missions, in their last letters, are most insistent upon. They are tired of dealing with the presidio, where the Officer does not absolutely refuse, but where repairs are done very slowly, and, all too frequently, a bad job is made of them. With a blacksmith in San Diego, the missions nearby can be served from there, and the one in Carmel can serve those of San Antonio and San Luis.

I beg of Your Excellency that, for the setting up of the two said forges, you order that there be sent and delivered to the two missions a goodly supply of iron—mostly in bars, partly in sheets—and that it be clearly stated that it be sent for the missions. In that way, so as to get possession of it, we will avoid any further difficulties or counterclaims on the part of the presidio.

We are in as much need of two carpenters as we are of two blacksmiths, one for the missions near Monterey, and the other to be located at Mission San Gabriel de los Temblores, where San Diego and San Buenaventura can make use of him. Both of them should come equipped with the tools of their trade. All of these matters could easily be attended to, if Your Excellency would give whatever orders seem suitable to you to someone in Guadalaxara. There could easily be sent from there the two blacksmiths, the two carpenters, and all of their equipment. But they should be clearly given to understand that the equipment is not their own, but the property of the respective missions. . . .

It seems to me that it would be most helpful if Your Excellency were to give strict orders to the said Commissary at San Blas, that he take greater care than he has till now taken in the packing of provisions forwarded for the maintenance of these missions and presidio. If the corn is put on board when it has already been attacked by grubs, and is full of maggots—and the same goes for the rest of the supplies—what will be its state when it arrvies at its destination, and what condition will it be in when the time comes to eat it? The corn that has been on board fresh and in good condition has arrived there in the same good condition. But sometimes, when we received it with the kernels empty, the Captain of the boat answered that that was the way it was loaded in San Blas. Last year there was no meat; and this year, what did come, besides being small in quantity, was so maggoty and putrid that very reasonably it was said to be the same that was to have come the year before; and not having much room in the boat, our meat supply was neither much, nor little, but nil.

There is nothing in greater abundance in the countryside around San Blas than herds of cows. Counting this year, it will now be two years since our poor men have been promised—ever since we got there—as part of their daily ration, half a pound or six ounces of meat. They have practically not tasted any other meat than what they have obtained from the gentiles or from hunting.

But, this last year the greatest pity of all has been concerning the flour, which is, of all the things that are sent us, or may be sent, the most helpful and most basic for the sustenance of life. It was put in plain sacks of poor material made of burlap or hemp, and consequently ran out at every motion or contact; and so the assignments arrived minus much that should have been there. And it is not hard to picture how much more they would be diminished when, after a lengthy journey, they arrived at their respective missions. How much money is thus thrown to the winds, both for what is lost—of the better quality—and for what is saved! If Your Excellency would kindly order the said article to be sent under the same stipulations that the Most Excellent Marqués de Croix laid down, such great losses would be avoided; and, with the same number of boatloads, there would be food to eat for a much longer time. . . .

I also ask Your Excellency that you allow a bounty for those, be they soldiers or not, who enter into the state of marriage with girls of that faraway country, new Christian converts. On that point, the Most Illustrious Inspector General gave repeated orders to Don Pedro Fages, but I was not able to ascertain the exact terms and conditions. However, whatever the case may be, it seems to me that anyone who marries after this fashion should be allowed to stay permanently attached to his wife's mission, without being removed to another; that he should be allowed an animal, immediately for his own use, if he is without one; and that, after he has worked a year or more on the mission farms, he be given from the royal herd two cows and a mule, or whatever may appear most suitable to Your Excellency. Lastly that, as time goes on, he might be assigned a piece of land for his own personal use provided he has nothing else to fall back upon.

A LETTER FROM GENERAL GEORGE WASHINGTON
TO DIEGO DE GARDOQUI, 1786

> Source: Dario Fernández Flores, The Spanish
> Heritage in the United States. Madrid: Servicio
> Informativo Español, 1971.

Sir

The letter which your Excellency did me the favor to write to me on the first of this month does me great honor; -- The sentiments which you have been pleased to entertain of my conduct are very flattering; and the friendly manner in which they are expressed is highly pleasing. To meet the approbation of a gentleman whose good wishes were early engaged in the American cause, & who has attended to its progress thro' the various stages of the revolution, must be considered as a happy circumstance for me; & I shall seek occasionally to testify my sense of it.

With much truth, I repeat the assurances offered to your Excellency thro' Mr. Banden, of the pleasure I should have in seeing you at my seat in this State, that I might express personally to you, how sensibly I feel for the proposed honor of your correspondence, & pray you to offer in such terms as you know would be most acceptable & proper, my gratitude to His Catholic Majesty, for his royal present to me, than which nothing could have been more flattering or valuable.

> With much esteem, respect & consideration
> I have the honor to be, Excelly.
> G. Washington.

Mount Vernon.
20th January, 1786.

FLORIDA TREATY
1819

Ratified February 22, 1819, the Florida Treaty provided the agreement by which Apain ceded its Florida territory to the United States.

Source: Henry Steele Commager, ed., Documents of American History, eighth edition, p. 224. New York: Appleton-Century-Crofts, Inc., 1968. Copyright 1968 by the Meredith Corporation.

. . . ART. II. His Catholic Majesty cedes to the United States, in full property and sovereignty, all the territories which belonged to him, situated to the eastward of the Mississippi, known by the name of East and West Florida. The adjacent islands dependent on said provinces, all public lots and squares, vacant lands, public edifices, fortifications, barracks, and other buildings, which are not private property, archives and documents, which relate directly to the property and sovereignty of said provinces, are included in this article. . . .

ART. III. The boundary line between the two countries, west of the Mississippi, shall begin on the Gulph of Mexico, at the mouth of the river Sabine, in the sea, continuing north, along the western bank of that river, to the 32d degree of latitude; thence, by a line due north, to the degree of latitude where it strikes the Rio Roxo of Natchitoches, or Red River; thence following the course of the Rio Roxo westward, to the degree of longitude 100 west from London and 23 from Washington; then, crossing the said Red River, and running thence, by a line due north, to the river Arkansas, thence, following the course of the southern bank of the Arkansas, to its source,

in latitude 42 north; and thence, by that parallel of latitude, to the South Sea. The whole being as laid down in Melish's map of the United States, published at Philadelphia, improved to the first of January, 1818. But if the source of the Arkansas River shall be found to fall north or south of latitude 42, then the line shall run from the said source due north or south, as the case may be, till it meets the said parallel of latitude 42, and thence, along the said parallel, to the South Sea: All the islands in the Sabine, and the said Red and Arkansas Rivers, throughout the course thus described, to belong to the United States; but the use of the waters, and the navigation of the Sabine to the sea, and of the said rivers Roxo and Arkansas, throughout the extent of the said boundary, on their respective banks, shall be common to the respective inhabitants of both nations. . . .

ART. V. The inhabitants of the ceded territories shall be secured in the free exercise of their religion, without any restriction. . . .

ART. VI. The inhabitants of the territories which His Catholic Majesty cedes to the United States, by this treaty, shall be incorporated in the Union of the United States, as soon as may be consistent with the principles of the Federal Constitution, and admitted to the enjoyment of all the privileges, rights, and immunities of the citizens of the United States. . . .

ART. XI. The United States, exonerating Spain from all demands in future, on account of the claims of their citizens to which the renunciations herein contained extend, and considering them entirely cancelled, undertake to make satisfaction for the same, to an amount not exceeding five millions of dollars. To ascertain the full amount and validity of those claims, a commission, to consist of three Commissioners, citizens of the United States, shall be appointed by the President, by and with the advice and consent of the Senate. . . .

ART. XV. Spanish vessels, laden only with productions of Spanish growth or manufacture, coming directly from Spain, or her colonies, "shall be admitted, for the term of twelve years, to the ports of Pensacola and St. Augustine, without paying other or higher duties on their cargoes, or of tonnage, than will be paid by the vessels of the United States. During the said term no other nation shall enjoy the same privileges within the ceded territories. . . .

A PROCLAMATION ON PUBLIC EDUCATION IN NEW MEXICO
1836

In 1836, Albino Perez, governor of New Mexico,
issued a proclamation calling for the establishment of public education in New Mexico.

Source: Ralph Emerson Twitchell, The Leading
Facts of New Mexican History, vol. II, pp. 57-59.
Cedar Rapids, Iowa: 1912.

Ignorance, and idleness, have always been the cause of infinite evil
among men in society, and to diminish them, the only remedy and
the most efficacious adopted in all countries of the world, is the
education of Youth. In this valuable and interesting province securing the good of the people being the principal object, the true lovers
of the public weal should attend to this, and it is also the most
sacred obligation of the local authorities. This important branch is
in a sad state throughout the territory, and more especially in this
capital, which by its very nature and elements, does not think
profoundly on the means to overcome these false difficulties, which
seem by their continuation, to justify the neglect. Running the
streets are children who ought to be receiving the education so
necessary at the fitting and proper age; youths of evil disposition,
abandoned to laziness and licentiousness, practicing vices; useless
aims which only serve to corrupt, like the plague, the city that
tolerates and feeds them; and above all, what are the results? Rob-
bery, immorality, poverty, desertion, and the most humiliating
shame of the city, which if it were cared for by its municipal
authorities, should be the enviable example of others composing
a most interesting part of the Mexican Nation.

Moved by such salutary reflections, and the love I bear to the
inhabitants of this soil, and by the obligation imposed upon me
by my position, I issue for the relief of the Royal Municipality the
following Plan of Regulation of Public Instruction.

Art. 1. There shall be in this city two schools, particularly of
primary instruction, in charge of Masters who may present themselves to conduct them, and who have the proper capacity in the
judgment of a commission named by the corporation, which shall

examine them in reading, writing, and counting.

2. The schools of the same nature now existing, gone through by heads of families, shall be destroyed, provided always that the Masters who conduct them have not the capacity and the approval required by the preceding article, to which end they may present themselves for examination, in opposition.

3. The Masters shall enjoy such salary or recompense as may be agreed upon with the heads of families, and shall receive pay from those known to be poor, in products of the soil, teaching gratis, orphan children, or those of the absolutely miserable, who have no livelihood or power to pay.

4. All Fathers or Guardians who have children in their care from the age of five to twelve years, are obliged to send them to one of the schools whichever best suits them, and the youths of twelve years or more [must be] in houses of artisans in the different branches of industry, that they may earn a living by honest occupation.

5. Those who fail to comply with the first part of the preceding article, by omission or neglect, shall be required by law, to pay a fine of from, one to five p. according to their means, in the first, double in the second, and triple in the third, and those who are still recalcitrant, and those who cannot pay the fine, shall be punished by law with three days arrest, doubling this punishment in the same way as the pecuniary one.

6. The Youths spoken of in the second part of the fourth article who do not consent to learn a trade, or who have no honest occupation, shall be treated as vagrant or vicious, and be tried and sentenced by the established Court and the laws governing such cases.

7. The Justices of the Wards, the wardens or deputies of the police, may arrest youths of twelve years or over, whom they find in the streets and public places engaged in betting games, at the end of eight days giving notice to one of the magistrates for the recognizance; and the children of twelve or under whom they find behaving ill, they shall take to the school that they may there suffer the same penalty of detention, advising the Master to punish them without fail.

8. Every one or two wards shall form two blocks proportionately, and designated by known names and fixed numbers.

9. To facilitate the better carrying out of this proclamation there shall be in each block a commissioner of Public Instruction, named by three justices unanimously whose duties shall be;

First. To make exact lists of the inhabitants of their blocks, with a statement of ages and occupations by which they live.

Second. To make another list of the children who shall attend the school, and go to each of the two, in order to learn if they are there; an account of the youths who ought to apply themselves to a trade, in what shop and with what Masters, and of the day laborers and where, they work, so that they can certify to the correctness of all this.

Third. To announce, courteously, one, two, or three times, to the fathers of families or guardians of children, what is set forth in the clauses of the preceding articles.

Fourth. To give notice in writing, to the magistrate of the precinct of those who, having been admonished, still do not comply, so that through him, or by advising the judge, the law may inflict the penalty, to which they have made themselves liable.

Fifth. To give notice, in the same manner, of all those living in idleness, who, having been admonished, do not find occupation, declaring all they can testify as to the proper or objectionable habits of the individuals.

Sixth. To give notice also, of any suspicious persons that may be in their blocks, who are spending money without knowing whether they come by it honestly, with the grounds for the suspicion.

Seventh. To visit every month, the schools to which the children go, to learn from the Masters whether they attend, and to get the information for their guidance. Similar visits shall be made to the workshops for the same purpose.

Eighth. They shall make note, in their lists, of the inhabitants who leave their blocks, to what others they go, and of those who come to live in their own.

Ninth. They shall be charged with the cleanliness of the streets and public places in their blocks, giving to the magistrate of the precinct of any neglect they notice.

Art. 10. Any person interfering with the commissioner in the discharge of his duty, shall be punished by a fine of from five to twenty-five p. without prejudice that if the fault be serious, he may be punished according to the laws relating to ordinary transgressions.

11. The duty of a commissioner of Public Instruction shall be a compulsory one, and no one can be excused from discharging it; it is obligatory for six months, without being required to continue, this term completed, until the end of the year, and the magistrates can remove him, for sufficient cause as neglect or bad management, if proven.

12. For any offense committed by the commissioner in the discharge of his duties, he shall be punished by a fine of from ten to thirty p. and deprivation of duty; and if the offence be the concealment of mischievous persons, or the toleration of them without giving notice to the Judges there shall be exacted fifty p. or two months forced labor.

13. This ordinance may be amended in whole or in part when the R. Ayuntamiento may deem proper, being convinced of its advantages or invalidity.

THE TREATY OF GUADALUPE HIDALGO
1848

The Treaty of Guadalupe Hidalgo, concluded on
February 2, 1848, ended the war between the
United States and Mexico.

Source: Hunter Miller, ed., Treaties and Other
International Acts of the United States of America,
vol. V, pp. 207-236. Washington, D.C.: Government Printing Office, 1937.

In the name of Almighty God:
    The United States of America, and the United Mexican States,
animated by a sincere desire to put an end to the calamities of the
war which unhappily exists between the two Republics, and to
establish upon a solid basis relations of peace and friendship, which
shall confer reciprocal benefits upon the citizens of both, and assure
the concord, harmony and mutual confidence, wherein the two peoples should live, as good neighbours, have for that purpose appointed their respective Plenipotentiaries: that is to say, the President of the United States has appointed Nicholas P. Trist, a citizen
of the United States, and the President of the Mexican Republic has
appointed Don Luis Gonzaga Cuevas, Don Bernardo Couto, and Don
Miguel Atristain, citizens of the said Republic; who, after a reciprocal communication of their respective full powers, have, under
the protection of Almighty God, the author of Peace, arranged,
agreed upon, and signed the following
    Treaty of Peace, Friendship, Limits and Settlement between the
United States of America and the Mexican Republic.

Article I.

    There shall be firm and universal peace between the United States
of America and the Mexican Republic, and between their respective
countries, territories, cities, towns and people, without exception of
places or persons.

Article II.

Immediately upon the signature of this Treaty, a convention shall be entered into between a Commissioner or Commissioners appointed by the General in Chief of the forces of the United States, and such as may be appointed by the Mexican Government, to the end that a provisional suspension of hostilities shall take place, and that, in the places occupied by the said forces, constitutional order may be reestablished, as regards the political, administrative, and judicial branches, so far as this shall be permitted by the circumstances of military occupation. . . .

Article V.

The Boundary line between the two Republics shall commence in the Gulf of Mexico, three leagues from land, opposite the mouth of the Rio Grande, otherwise called Rio Bravo del Norte, or opposite the mouth of it's deepest branch, if it should have more than one branch emptying directly into the sea; from thence, up the middle of that river, following the deepest channel, where it has more than one, to the point where it strikes the southern boundary of New Mexico; thence, westwardly, along the whole southern boundary of New Mexico (which runs north of the town called *Paso*) to it's western termination; thence, northward, along the western line of New Mexico, until it intersects the first branch of the river Gila; (or if it should not intersect any branch of that river, then, to the point on the said line nearest to such branch, and thence in a direct line to the same;) thence down the middle of the said branch and of the said river, until it empties into the Rio Colorado; thence, across the Rio Colorado, following the division line between Upper and Lower California, to the Pacific Ocean.

The southern and western limits of New Mexico, mentioned in this Article, are those laid down in the Map, entitled *"Map of the United Mexican States, as organized and defined by various acts of the Congress of said Republic, and constructed according to the best Authorities. Revised Edition. Published at New York in 1847 by J. Disturnell:"* of which Map a Copy is added to this treaty, bearing the signatures and seals of the Undersigned Plenipotentiaries. And, in order to preclude all difficulty in tracing upon the ground the limit separating Upper from Lower California, it is agreed that the said limit shall consist of a straight line, drawn from the middle of the Rio Gila, where it unites with the Colorado, to a point on the coast of the Pacific Ocean, distant one marine league due south of the southernmost point of the Port of San Diego, according to the plan of said port, made in the year 1782 by Don Juan Pantoja, second sailing master of the Spanish fleet, and published at Madrid in the year 1802, in the Atlas to the voyage of the schooners *Sutil* and *Mexicana:* of which plan a copy is hereunto added, signed and sealed by the respective plenipotentiaries.

In order to designate the Boundary line with due precision, upon authoritative maps, and to establish upon the ground landmarks which shall allow the limits of both Republics, as described in the present Article, the two Governments shall each appoint a Commissioner and a Surveyor, who, before the expiration of one year from the date of the exchange of ratifications of this treaty, shall meet at the Port of San Diego, and proceed to run and mark the said boundary in it's whole course, to the Mouth of the Rio Bravo del Norte. They shall keep journals and make out plans of their operations; and the result, agreed upon by them, shall be deemed a part of this Treaty, and shall have the same force as if it were inserted therein. The two Governments will amicably agree regarding what may be necessary to these persons, and also as to their respective escorts, should such be necessary.

The Boundary line established by this Article shall be religiously respected by each of the two Republics, and no change shall ever be made therein, except by the express and free consent of both nations, lawfully given by the General Government of each, in conformity with it's own constitution.

Article VI.

The Vessels and citizens of the United States shall, in all time, have a free and uninterrupted passage by the Gulf of California, and by the River Colorado below it's confluence with the Gila, to and from their possessions situated north of the Boundary line defined in the preceding Article: it being understood, that this passage is to be by navigating the Gulf of California and the River Colorado, and not by land, without the express consent of the Mexican Government.

If, by the examinations which may be made, it should be ascertained to be practicable and advantageous to construct a road, canal or railway, which should, in whole or in part, run upon the river Gila, or upon it's right or it's left bank, within the space of one marine league from either margin of the river, the Governments of both Republics will form an agreement regarding it's construction, in order that it may serve equally for the use and advantage of both countries.

Article VII.

The river Gila, and the part of the Rio Bravo del Norte lying below the southern boundary of New Mexico, being, agreeably to the fifth Article, divided in the middle between the two Republics, the navigation of the Gila and of the Bravo below said boundary shall be free and common to the vessels and citizens of both countries; and neither shall, without the consent of the other, construct any work that may impede or interrupt, in whole or in part, the exercise of this right: not even for the purpose of favouring new methods of navigation. Nor shall any tax or contribution, under any denomination or title, be levied upon vessels or persons navigating the same, or upon merchandise or effects transported thereon, except in the case of landing upon one of their shores. If, for the purpose of making the said rivers navigable, or for maintaining them in such state, it should be necessary or advantageous to establish any tax or contribution, this shall not be done without the consent of both Governments.

The stipulations contained in the present Article shall not impair the territorial rights of either Republic, within it's established limits.

Article VIII.

Mexicans now established in territories previously belonging to Mexico, and which remain for the future within the limits of the United States, as defined by the present treaty, shall be free to continue where they now reside, or to remove at any time to the Mexican Republic, retaining the property which they possess in the said territories, or disposing thereof, and removing the proceeds wherever they please; without their being subjected, on this account, to any contribution, tax or charge whatever.

Those who shall prefer to remain in the said territories, may either retain the title and rights of Mexican citizens, or acquire those of citizens of the United States. But they shall be under the obligation to make their election within one year from the date of the exchange of ratifications of this treaty: and those who shall remain in the said territories, after the expiration of that year, without having declared their intention to retain the character of Mexicans, shall be considered to have elected to become citizens of the United States.

In the said territories, property of every kind, now belonging to Mexicans, not established there, shall be inviolably respected. The present owners, the heirs of these, and all Mexicans who may hereafter acquire said property by contract, shall enjoy with respect to it, guaranties equally ample as if the same belonged to citizens of the United States.

Article IX.

The Mexicans who, in the territories aforesaid, shall not preserve the character of citizens of the Mexican Republic, conformably with what is stipulated in the preceding article, shall be incorporated into the Union of the United States and be admitted, at the proper time (to be judged of by the Congress of the United States) to the enjoyment of all the rights of citizens of the United States according to the principles of the Constitution; and in the mean time shall be maintained and protected in the free enjoyment of their liberty and property, and secured in the free exercise of their religion without restriction.

[One of the amendments of the Senate struck out Article 10.]

Article XI.

Considering that a great part of the territories which, by the present Treaty, are to be comprehended for the future within the limits of the United States, is now occupied by savage tribes, who will hereafter be under the exclusive controul of the Government of the United States, and whose incursions within the territory of Mexico would be prejudicial in the extreme; it is solemnly agreed that all such incursions shall be forcibly restrained by the Government of the United States, whensoever this may be necessary; and that when they cannot be prevented, they shall be punished by the said Government, and satisfaction for the same shall be exacted: all in the same way, and with equal diligence and energy, as if the same incursions were meditated or committed within it's own territory against it's own citizens.

It shall not be lawful, under any pretext whatever, for any inhabitant of the United States, to purchase or acquire any Mexican or any foreigner residing in Mexico, who may have been captured by Indians inhabiting the territory of either of the two Republics, nor to purchase or acquire horses, mules, cattle or property of any kind, stolen within Mexican territory by such Indians.

And, in the event of any person or persons, captured within Mexican Territory by Indians, being carried into the territory of the United States, the Government of the latter engages and binds itself in the most solemn manner, so soon as it shall know of such captives being within it's territory, and shall be able so to do, through the faithful exercise of it's influence and power, to rescue them and return them to their country, or deliver them to the agent or representative of the Mexican Government. The Mexican Authorities will, as far as practicable, give to the Government of the United States notice of such captures; and it's agent shall pay the expenses incurred in the maintenance and transmission of the rescued captives; who, in the mean time, shall be treated with the utmost hospitality by the American authorities at the place where they may be. But if the Government of the United States, before receiving such notice from Mexico, should obtain intelligence through any other channel, of the existence of Mexican captives within it's territory, it will proceed forthwith to effect their release and delivery to the Mexican agent, as above stipulated.

For the purpose of giving to these stipulations the fullest possible efficacy, thereby affording the security and redress demanded by their true spirit and intent, the Government of the United States will now and hereafter pass, without unnecessary delay, and always vigilantly enforce, such laws as the nature of the subject may require. And finally, the sacredness of this obligation shall never be lost sight of by the said Government, when providing for the removal of the Indians from any portion of the said territories, or for it's being settled by citizens of the United States; but on the contrary special care shall then be taken not to place it's Indian occupants under the necessity of seeking new homes, by committing those invasions which the United States have solemnly obliged themselves to restrain.

Article XII.

In consideration of the extension acquired by the boundaries of the United States, as defined in the fifth Article of the present Treaty, the Government of the United States engages to pay to that of the Mexican Republic the sum of fifteen Millions of Dollars.

TREATY OF PEACE WITH SPAIN
1898

Signed December 10, 1898, this treaty concluded
the Spanish-American War. By its provisions
Spain ceded Puerto Rico to the United States and
relinquished its political authority over Cuba.

Source: Henry Steele Commager, ed., Documents
of American History, eighth edition, pp. 7-8.
New York: Appleton-Century-Crofts, Inc., 1968.

ART. I. Spain relinquishes all claim of sovereignty over and title to Cuba.

And as the island is, upon its evacuation by Spain, to be occupied by the United States, the United States will, so long as such occupation shall last, assume and discharge the obligations that may under international law result from the fact of its occupation, for the protection of life and property.

ART. II. Spain cedes to the United States the island of Porto Rico and other islands now under Spanish sovereignty in the West Indies, and the island of Guam in the Marianas or Ladrones.

ART. III. Spain cedes to the United States the archipelago known as the Philippine Islands, and comprehending the islands lying within the following line:

A line running from west to east along or near the twentieth parallel of north latitude, and through the middle of the navigable channel of Bachi, from the one hundred and eighteenth (118th) to the one hundred and twenty seventh (127th) degree meridian of longitude east of Greenwich, thence along the one hundred and twenty seventh (127th) degree meridian of longitude east of Greenwich to the parallel of four degrees and forty five minutes (4° 45') north latitude, thence along the parellel of four degrees and forty five minutes (4° 45') north latitude to its intersection with the meridian of longitude one hundred and nineteen degrees and thirty five minutes (119° 35') east of Greenwich, thence along the meridian of longitude one hundred and nineteen degrees and thirty five minutes (119° 35') east of Greenwich to the parallel of latitude seven degrees and forty minutes (7° 40') north, thence along the parallel of latitude seven degrees and forty minutes (7° 40') north to its intersection with the one hundred and sixteenth (116th) degree meridian of longitude east of Greenwich, thence by a direct line to the intersection of the tenth (10th) degree parallel of north latitude with the one hundred and eighteenth (118th) degree meridian of longitude east of Greenwich, and thence along the one hundred and eighteenth (118th) degree meridian of longitude east of Greenwich to the point of beginning.

The United States will pay to Spain the sum of twenty million dollars ($20,000,000) within three months after the exchange of the ratifications of the present treaty.

ART. IV. The United States will, for the

term of ten years from the date of the exchange of the ratifications of the present treaty, admit Spanish ships and merchandise to the ports of the Philippine Islands on the same terms as ships and merchandise of the United States. . . .

ART. VII. The United States and Spain mutually relinquish all claims for indemnity, national and individual, of every kind, of either Government, or of its citizens or subjects, against the other Government, that may have arisen since the beginning of the late insurrection in Cuba and prior to the exchange of ratifications of the present treaty, including all claims for indemnity for the cost of the war.

The United States will adjudicate and settle the claims of its citizens against Spain relinquished in this article.

ART. VIII. In conformity with the provisions of Articles I, II, and III of this treaty, Spain relinquishes in Cuba, and cedes in Porto Rico and other islands in the West Indies,

in the island of Guam, and in the Philippine Archipelago, all the buildings, wharves, barracks, forts, structures, public highways and other immovable property which, in conformity with law, belong to the public domain, and as such belong to the Crown of Spain.

And it is hereby declared that the relinquishment or cession, as the case may be, to which the preceding paragraph refers, cannot in any respect impair the property or rights which by law belong to the peaceful possession of property of all kinds, of provinces, municipalities, public or private establishments, ecclesiastical or civic bodies, or any other associations having legal capacity to acquire and possess property in the aforesaid territories renounced or ceded, or of private individuals, of whatsoever nationality such individuals may be.

The aforesaid relinquishment or cession, as the case may be, includes all documents exclusively referring to the sovereignty relinquished or ceded that may exist in the archives of the Peninsula. Where any document in such archives only in part relates to said sovereignty, a copy of such part will be furnished whenever it shall be requested. Like rules shall be reciprocally observed in favor of Spain in respect of documents in the archives of the islands above referred to.

In the aforesaid relinquishment or cession, as the case may be, are also included such rights as the Crown of Spain and its authorities possess in respect of the official archives and records, executive as well as judicial, in the islands above referred to, which relate to said islands or the rights and property of their inhabitants. Such archives and records shall be carefully preserved, and private persons shall without distinction have the right to require, in accordance with law, authenticated copies of the contracts, wills and other instruments forming part of notarial protocols or files, or which may be contained in the executive or judicial archives, be the latter in Spain or in the islands aforesaid. . . .

ART. X. The inhabitants of the territories over which Spain relinquishes or cedes her sovereignty shall be secured in the free exercise of their religion.

ART. XI. The Spaniards residing in the territories over which Spain by this treaty cedes or relinquishes her sovereignty shall be subject in matters civil as well as criminal to the jurisdiction of the courts of the country wherein they reside, pursuant to the ordinary laws governing the same; and they shall have the right to appear before such courts, and to pursue the same course as citizens of the country to which the courts belong. . . .

ART. XIII. The rights of property secured by copyrights and patents acquired by Spaniards in the Island of Cuba, and in Porto Rico, the Philippines and other ceded territories, at the time of the exchange of the ratifications of this treaty, shall continue to be respected. Spanish scientific, literary and artistic works, not subversive of public order in the territories in question, shall continue to be admitted free of duty into such territories, for the period of ten years, to be reckoned from the date of the exchange of the ratifications of this treaty. . . .

ART. XV. The Government of each country will, for the term of ten years, accord to the merchant vessels of the other country the same treatment in respect of all port charges, including entrance and clearance dues, light dues, and tonnage duties, as it accords to its own merchant vessels, not engaged in the coastwise trade.

This article may at any time be terminated on six months' notice given by either Government to the other.

ART. XVI. It is understood that any obligations assumed in this treaty by the United States with respect to Cuba are limited to the time of its occupancy thereof; but it will upon the termination of such occupancy, advise any Government established in the island to assume the same obligations.

MEMOIRS OF MIGUEL ANTONIO OTERO
1935

In the following pages Miguel Antonio Otero,
former governor of the New Mexico Territory,
recalls his experiences on the American frontier.

Source: Miguel Antonio Otero, My Life on the
Frontier, pp. 210-18, 268-81. New York: The
Press of the Pioneers, 1935.

Chapter XIX

I SHALL close this recital of the turbulent year 1880 with
an incident near its end that caused Las Vegas to feel that it
was a participant in the lawlessness then rampant in the
southern part of the Territory and that brought back to its
notice Dave Rudabaugh.

Early on the morning of December 23, 1880, at the little
rock house built many years before by Alejandro Perea, near
Stinking Springs, N. Mex., Pat F. Garrett, Frank Stewart,
Lon Chambers, Lee Hall, Louis Bozeman (alias "The
Animal"), James H. East, Barney Mason, Tom Emory
(known as "Poker Tom"), and Bob Williams (alias "Ten-
derfoot Bob") killed Charlie Bowdre and captured Billy the
Kid, Dave Rudabaugh, Billy Wilson and Tom Pickett.

The Kid and his companions had taken refuge in the rock
house when they felt closing around them the toils of Pat
Garrett's determined effort to capture the party. Garrett's
posse had besieged the rock house all during the night, and
when Charlie Bowdre appeared at the door early the next
morning, Garrett had given unmistakable indication of the
temper of the quest, by shooting Bowdre, who died in a few

minutes. So the Kid and the remaining three of his company
decided to propose terms of surrender, which Garrett agreed
upon, promising them protection until they could be tried.

In seeking a jail strong enough to hold the quartet, Garrett naturally turned toward Santa Fé, and as the nearest
railroad station was East Las Vegas, he carried his prisoners
there. The news that these noted desperadoes were coming
through Las Vegas, and perhaps would be kept overnight in
the Las Vegas jail, brought large numbers of curious people
to the plaza.

Albert E. Hyde, who was in Las Vegas at the time, wrote
a magazine article some years ago, giving a graphic eye-
witness account of the entry of Garrett's party. As this tallies
with what I remember, I shall reproduce it:

It was a beautiful afternoon, and the elevation of the Grand
View Hotel afforded a wide range of vision across the plains,
stretching to the blue line of distant hills.

As the hours passed, the crowds began to grow more impatient
and distrustful. All had become skeptical, when from our point of
vantage we discerned a cloud of dust in the southwest. When the
cause of it advanced close enough for the people to descry a wagon
outfit accompanied by mounted men, a mighty shout went up. The
good news was indeed true. Billy the Kid was a prisoner and Pat
Garrett was a hero.

As the wagon, pulled by four mules, approached, we saw four
men sitting in the bed, two on a side, facing each other. The Kid,
whom Dr. Sutfin had known in his cowboy days and instantly
recognized, was on the hotel side of the wagon, chained to a fierce-
looking, dark-bearded man who kept his slouch hat pulled well down
over his eyes, and looked neither to the right nor to the left. This
man was the daring and dangerous Dave Rudabaugh, who, among
many other crimes, had killed the Mexican jailor at Las Vegas a short
time before. He feared recognition, as well he might, for the Mexican population thirsted for his blood. The other two prisoners were
Pickett and Wilson, prominent members of the Kid's gang.

Billy the Kid was in a joyous mood. He was a short, slender, beardless young man. The marked peculiarity of his face was a pointed chin and a short upper lip which exposed the large front teeth and gave a chronic grin to his expression. He wore his hat pushed far back, and jocularly greeted the crowd. Recognizing Dr. Sutfin he called: "Hello, Doc! Thought I'd jes' drop in an' see how you fellers in Vegas air behavin' yerselves."

Heavily armed deputies rode on each side of the wagon, with two bringing up the rear. Garrett rode in front. The large crowd evidently surprised and annoyed him. Fearing for the safety of Rudabaugh, he turned and gave a low order to the mule-driver, who instantly whipped up his team, and a run was made across the plaza to the jail.

Garrett heard enough during the next few hours to convince him that an attempt would be made to lynch Rudabaugh. He promptly increased his force to thirty men, who guarded the jail that night. In the meantime he planned to take the prisoners next day to Santa Fé for safe-keeping. Not a suspicion of this move was allowed to get out.

Garrett placed his prisoners in the jail for the night. The next morning he began preparations to move them to Santa Fé by the railroad. But he experienced considerable trouble in getting the San Miguel officials to allow him to take Rudabaugh along, for local sentiment was strong for keeping the latter in Las Vegas now that he was back on the scene of his crime. Garrett protested that he held his prisoners under a United States warrant and that this fact gave him a precedence over the local officials. But the Las Vegas officers were not inclined to yield.

Finally, despite the mutterings of the Las Vegas people, Garrett placed the four prisoners in a closed carriage and hurried them to the railroad depot in the New Town, where he found a mob assembled, the majority of whom were armed with rifles and pistols. Sympathetic with the mob were the sheriff, Desiderio Romero, and his deputies, headed by his brother, Pablo Romero, generally called "Colorow" on account of his red hair and heavy, bushy, red mustache and chin whiskers. The demand that Dave Rudabaugh be turned over to the Las Vegas officers was renewed, and again Garrett refused.

He had managed by this time to get his prisoners aboard the train and had them in one car under a heavy guard consisting of Cosgrove, Stewart and Mason. The mob surrounded the depot and train, and showed signs of forcing its way into the car where the prisoners were held. But Garrett stood on the platform, calmly, and said: "I promised these men I would deliver them to the sheriff of Santa Fé County or to the United States officer at Santa Fé, and I intend to do exactly as I promised. Now, if you people insist on trying to take them away from me, I can see only one thing for me to do and that is to arm every one of them and turn them loose to defend themselves as best they may. And what is more, all my officers and myself will assist in protecting them."

As Garrett finished talking, my father got up on the car-platform and stood beside him. He first shook Garrett's hand, and then turning to the sheriff and his deputies, as well as to the mob, said: "Gentlemen, these prisoners are in the custody of Mr. Garrett, and he has given his word that he will turn them over to the proper authorities at Santa Fé. This I know he will do. Now, it is a very serious thing for you men to hold up the United States mail as you are doing, and as the train is ready to start, I appeal to you, as your friend, to retire at once; otherwise the consequences may be very severe. I will give you my personal guaranty that Mr. Garrett will do exactly as he has said. The judge of this judicial district resides in Santa Fé, and on their arrival there, he will immediately take full charge."

This speech had the desired effect. The officers and the mob withdrew, and the train, which had been held up for about an hour, pulled out on its way to Santa Fé. While the mob was holding the train and seemed determined to take

Rudabaugh away from the officers, Pat Garrett stepped back into the car. To the prisoners Garrett said: "Do not be uneasy. We are going to fight if they try to enter this car, and if the fight comes off I will arm you and allow you to take a hand." Rudabaugh was excited and considerably worried, but not so Billy the Kid. At Garrett's promise, the Kid's face beamed and his eyes fairly glistened, and he replied: "All right, Pat; all I want is a six-shooter. There is no danger though; those fellows won't fight."

I really believe, however, that the Kid was disappointed that the mob did not attack the car, for it would have unquestionably resulted in an opportunity for him to escape. Undoubtedly he had many friends among the crowd, for it was well known that he was on good terms with the native element of the country and had protected and helped them in every possible way. In return the native citizens were ready to do all in their power to assist him. If there had been an attack, the chances are that Garrett and his companions would have been killed in their effort to keep their prisoners. Rudabaugh would have fallen into the hands of the mob, and possibly lynching would have followed. But the quick and elusive Kid would probably have lost himself in the crowd and disappeared from the scene. My brother and I were so much interested in the whole thing that we secured permission from my father to go along on the train to Santa Fé, and we enjoyed ourselves immensely in the company of Garrett and his guards and their prisoners. On the way over, we talked much with Billy the Kid and Rudabaugh. The latter we knew quite well, as he had been on the police force in East Las Vegas for a time together with Mysterious Dave Mathers. The Kid we had never seen before, though we were of course familiar with his part in the Lincoln County War and in the reign of terror he had afterward created.

During our stay in Santa Fé, we were allowed to visit the Kid many times at the jail, taking him cigarette papers and tobacco, as well as chewing gum, candy, pies and nuts, for he was very fond of sweets and asked us to bring him such things. My impression of the Kid was that he was just about the same, so far as general appearance went, as most boys of his age. Sitting very close to him in the railroad coach, I observed quite plainly his apparent interest in everything taking place inside and outside of the car in which we were riding. He seemed to be intent on some weighty matter involving himself, and possibly was at the time evolving plans as to what to do in the event of an attack by the mob.

To be frank, I found myself liking the Kid, and long before we had reached Santa Fé, nothing would have pleased me better than to have witnessed his escape. He had his share of good qualities: he was pleasant to meet; he had the reputation of always being kind and considerate to the old, the young, and the poor; he was loyal to his friends and, above all, loved his mother devotedly. He was simply unfortunate in starting life, and became the victim of circumstances. I had been told that Billy had an ungovernable temper; if so, I never saw it in evidence, for he was always in a pleasant humor when I happened to meet him. Mrs. Jaramillo at Fort Sumner said of him: "Billy was a good boy, but he was hounded by bad men who wanted to kill him, because they feared him, and of course he had to defend himself." Don Martin Chaves of Santa Fé said: "Billy was a man with a noble heart, and a perfect gentleman. He never killed a native citizen of New Mexico in all his career, and the men he killed, he simply had to in defense of his own life. He never had to borrow courage from any man as he had plenty of it himself. He was a brave man and did not know what fear meant. They had to sneak up on him at dead of night and then murder him."

Mrs. Jaramillo I have known for many years. She is a lovely woman, kind and gentle. Don Martin Chaves is a quiet, unassuming and kindly gentleman. He is well up in the seventies and is in perfectly good health today. Most of the older citizens of Santa Fé are well acquainted with him, and he holds the respect and esteem of everyone knowing him in his community. So the testimony of these two regarding the real character of the Kid carries considerable weight. My own personal impression corroborates that of these other persons. In looking back to my first meeting with Billy the Kid, I have no hesitancy in saying my impressions of him were most favorable ones, and I believe I can honestly say he was "a man more sinned against than sinning."

Dave Rudabaugh remained in jail at Santa Fé for a time and was then taken back to Las Vegas and tried for the killing of Antonio Lino, the jailor. The outcome was conviction and a sentence to be hung, but Rudabaugh escaped from jail and went to Old Mexico, where he got into serious difficulty by killing a Mexican officer. The man whom he killed was very popular, and his friends went after Rudabaugh in great numbers and with more success than did the friends of Lino. They finally surrounded him, and in the fight that ensued, Rudabaugh was killed. His head was cut off and carried on a long pole around the Mexican plaza where Rudabaugh's victim had lived. After this display, the head and the body were given to the vultures to devour, and the well-picked bones left to bleach on the hillside. Grim as was this ending, I am inclined to think it was deserved, for Rudabaugh was one of the most desperate men of those wild days.

Of this same period, another episode occurs to me, which I believe will be of interest. During the early days following the entrance of the railroad, there was a saloon located on the southeast corner of the plaza just where the old First National Bank building now stands in the Old Town of Las Vegas. The bartender in this saloon was a man named Charlie White, thought to have been a member of the gang hailing from Dodge City. Several rooms in the rear of the saloon were used for different kinds of gambling, and were run by a tough lot of confidence-men and crooks. The barroom itself was usually crowded with bums and cappers working in the interest of the gamblers.

During the year 1880, Doc Holliday arrived in Las Vegas from Dodge City. He was quite a noted character in those days. He had been a dentist in some small farming town in central Illinois, and had become involved in a love affair which terminated by his being jilted by the young lady for another gay Lothario, who had been introduced to the family by Doc himself. This became the turning point in his life, and he decided to "Go West" and take his chances with killers and bad men. To fulfill such an ambition, he wisely selected Dodge City as the best locality to acquire a thorough education in the manly art of self-defense. After he had made what he thought was a sufficient advancement to enable him to rate himself as expert on the draw, quick on the trigger, a perfect marksman with a gun or pistol, as well as an experienced horseman, he qualified at once for an appointment under the celebrated Earp Brothers, who had undertaken the job and did finally succeed in "cleaning up" the town of Tombstone, Ariz.

Holliday had had some serious difficulty with Charlie White back in Dodge City, which was the immediate cause of White's departure from that place, but Doc had traced him to Las Vegas and had promised himself that if he ever passed through that town while White was there, he would certainly pay him a visit. Being a man of his word he stopped off in Las Vegas while en route to Tombstone to join the Earp Brothers, simply to square matters with his enemy. Holliday had no sooner gotten off the train than he started out to discover White's whereabouts. After locating him, he went back to the New Town for his supper. This done, he took the shortest trail for the saloon on the plaza. Doc entered the saloon with a cocked revolver in his hand and began hostilities at once, without previously making his presence known. White was in the act of serving some thirsty customers, but recognizing his old enemy from Dodge City, he ducked behind the bar just in time, while the customers ducked to the floor. White quickly emerged with a six-shooter, and the duel began in dead earnest, many shots being exchanged at short distance without effect.

The meeting was so sudden that both participants were evidently somewhat off their accustomed good marksmanship, but finally White dropped to the floor. At first it was thought that the shot had killed him, and Holliday feeling that he had fulfilled his mission to Las Vegas, departed for

the New Town, to mingle with his old friends of Dodge City. A doctor was called at once for White, and it was found that while the bullet had only grazed the skin, it had been so near the spine as to stun him temporarily. He was up and around in a couple of hours as good as ever.

Doc Holliday remained a few days in Las Vegas before taking his departure for Arizona, and I met him quite frequently and found him to be a very likable fellow. After leaving Arizona he went to Colorado, where he died a natural death. White had evidently tired of frontier life for he left for his home in Boston on the very first train going East. No arrests were made. It was simply allowed to pass, as no one was interested in either Holliday or White, and the peace officers in Las Vegas were much too busy looking after their own games.

Chapter XXIII

THROUGHOUT these pages dealing with my own experiences on the frontier there has appeared in the background many times my father Don Miguel Antonio Otero (I). I have already given some indication of the long, distinguished service he rendered New Mexico prior to 1862, when he gave up politics in order to devote his whole attention to his business interests. I have also shown how he was called away from these when the Atchison, Topeka & Santa Fé Railroad Company started to build from Topeka, Kans., towards the Territory of New Mexico and desired his services in securing its right-of-way. To accomplish what was necessary, he had to be most of the time at the front, and such items in the *Daily Optic* as the following show his activity.

From the issue of December 11th, 1879:

Hon. Miguel A. Otero joined William B. Strong, General Manager of the A. T. & S. F. R., George O. Manchester, Assistant General Manager, J. F. Goddard, General Freight Agent, George B. Lake, Division Superintendent, A. A. Robinson, Chief Engineer, and many Directors from Boston, on a trip to the end of the track.

Again, from the issue of January 8th, 1880:

Governor Anthony and Hon. Miguel A. Otero came into Las Vegas one day early this week. They were looking after the interest of the N.M. & S.F.R.R., and departed again for the ancient city.

Also, from the issue of January 10th, 1880:

Governor Anthony, Hon. Miguel A. Otero and Judge Henry L. Waldo arrived from Santa Fé on last night's train, and went east to Boston to attend a Directors' meeting of the A.T. & S.F.R.R.

Finally, this from the *Daily Optic* of April 3rd, 1880:

"Hon. Miguel A. Otero, Vice-President of the New Mexico and

Southern Pacific Railroad, the Jay Gould of Montezuma, was met by an *Optic* Inquisitor this morning, and the following confab took place:—

REPORTER: "Back from the south, I see?"

MR. OTERO: "Yes, I have been to Albuquerque and Bernalillo."

REPORTER: "How is Albuquerque panning out?"

MR. OTERO: "The New Town, I suppose you mean. A town company has laid out more than a hundred acres in town lots, which are selling rapidly and many buildings are going up."

REPORTER: "When will the Santa Fé Railroad get there?"

MR. OTERO: "About Tuesday, the 6th instant, possibly a day sooner."

REPORTER: "How about the Atlantic and Pacific Railroad? Will they build out of Albuquerque soon?"

MR. OTERO: "Yes. The money has been secured and there will be little delay," etc., etc.

These several items from the newspaper have been given to show the activity of my father in the construction of the Atchison, Topeka & Santa Fé Railroad through New Mexico. I would not be putting it too strongly if I said that it was entirely through his personal influence that favorable legislation such as was desired by the railroad officials was secured from the Territorial Legislature. It was also largely through his prestige and effort that the right-of-way through the Territory needed by the Santa Fé Route was secured without any compensation being demanded of the railroad, not even by my father himself, who worked untiringly for the railroad from 1873 until his death.

On numerous occasions I acted as my father's secretary, and was present with him at a meeting held in Santa Fé when Governor George T. Anthony, William B. Strong and A. A. Robinson urged my father to submit a bill for his services, saying to him: "Don Miguel, your services would be hard to estimate, for they have been worth to the company many thousands of dollars. We think you ought to put in your bill accordingly, and we will take pleasure in approving it." My father positively declined to do what they suggested, his refusal being put in the short but sincere statement: "I was working for New Mexico, and I am satisfied if my Territory gets the benefit of my labors."

Although my father considered himself definitely out of politics, he was unable to escape one more plunge into the whirlpool, although cesspool might be a better appellation, considering the malodorousness of New Mexican politics even fifty years ago. In the summer of 1880 the politicians of the Territory were busy getting ready for the coming election in the fall. The Democrats in looking around for a suitable nominee for Delegate to Congress felt that my father was the most popular man they could find, and so without his having been at all active in the matter they nominated him by acclamation at the Territorial convention held during that summer at Santa Fé and sent a committee to notify him of this action (he being in Santa Fé at the time) and to invite him to come and address the convention.

When the committee called upon my father, he concluded that the only course open to him was to respond to the wish of his party so strikingly and strongly expressed. So he accompanied the committee back to the hall where the convention was in session and, on his entrance, received an ovation, the delegates standing on their seats and cheering for several minutes. When the demonstration ended, my father was introduced by the chairman of the committee and delivered a rousing speech, which worked the convention up to the highest pitch of enthusiasm, especially when in the peroration he accepted the nomination and promised a vigorous and successful campaign against the nominee of the Republicans, Mr. Tranquilino Luna.

The political pot boiled and seethed all during the summer and early fall, the election taking precedence of everything else in the Territory. Rumors of great frauds planned by the Republicans were rife on the streets of every town in the Territory, and the Democrats made preparations to do what they could to check such tactics. But their efforts were unavailing. When the election came off, the result showed that under any fair and honest count my father would have been declared elected by a handsome majority, but through the basest and most barefaced frauds ever practiced in any country, he was robbed of his victory, and Tranquilino Luna declared elected.

I happened to be sent to Socorro County to watch for evidence of fraudulent practices in the river precincts and to gain all the facts possible as to frauds in Valencia County, where it was said they voted the sheep; and I can speak knowingly of what really took place in that county and which was verified a considerable time after the election. There was a precinct in Valencia County which had been specially created for the sole purpose of stealing the election. The returns from this precinct gave Luna nearly a thousand votes, every one of which was dishonest and fraudulent, while my father secured not a single vote in the precinct. The newly created precinct turned out on investigation to be merely a sheep camp belonging to the Luna family. A few years later Jesus M. Luna, an older brother of Tranquilino, and I were talking over the election in his home at Los Lunas and he admitted to me that my father had been honestly elected, but declared unblushingly that they had to count his brother Tranquilino in by fair means or foul.

I heard Mr. Worth Keene, then a railroad contractor on the line of the Atlantic & Pacific, building west from Albuquerque, tell how he and his camp had contributed to the polling of those thousand votes. In the conversation I was one of the party who heard Mr. Keene telling Solomon Luna, another brother of Tranquilino, how he had carried out the instructions given him by the Republican organization of Valencia County, which were as follows: "You must send from your camp six of your men in a light spring wagon drawn by a good team of mules to the voting place. These men are to vote, and then they will be given a slip of paper from one of the judges of election on which is written six names, which they are to use when they next appear at the voting place. They must then return to the wagon and drive out behind one of the sand-hills in the vicinity of the ranch house being used as a voting place. After each one has selected one of the names on the paper they drive back to the voting place and again vote under the names given them. This same procedure must be kept up all day." "I sent six of my most reliable men and they continued voting from sunrise to sunset, at the end of which time they had cast nearly one thousand votes for Tranquilino Luna. As not a single Democrat ticket was in evidence of course none was voted." All during the story Solomon Luna was noticeably uneasy and worried, no doubt fearing that Worth Keene might tell something they had been holding back from the public. He tried hard to stop him without attracting my attention, but Keene went on with his story, giving full details and seemed apparently proud of the part he had taken in the unlawful act. Finally it reached the point where Solomon's embarrassment became too noticeable, so I said: "Let Worth finish his story, for I heard exactly the same story from your brother Jesus some time ago. Worth has evidently forgotten that it was my father who was running against Tranquilino at the time." There was a death-like silence for several minutes, broken by Solomon inviting us all to take a drink.

What was done in Valencia County was but a sample of what was done by the Republican Party throughout the entire Territory. At the time my father was urged by many of his friends to bring a contest, for the general opinion was that this was one of the most daring and outrageous cases of stealing an election ever perpetrated in New Mexico or else-

where. But such a contest would have had to be fought out
before Congress, and as the House of Representatives was
then in the hands of the Republicans, my father thought it
useless to go to the trouble and expense of a contest. His
feelings were, however, so strong about the matter that I
believe had he lived until the next election he would have
been willing to enter the fray again and try conclusions with
Mr. Tranquilino Luna. It is true that he would in all likeli-
hood have encountered the same chicanery and fraud that
again resulted in the defeat of the Democratic candidate,
Francisco A. Manzanares, but he might have felt encouraged
to make a contest as did Manzanares. The complexion of the
House of Representatives had changed by that time and was
Democratic, so when the frauds and stealings were shown,
Francisco A. Manzanares secured his seat, to the entire satis-
faction of the people of New Mexico.

The first telephone company to organize and do business
in New Mexico was organized by my father, Page B. Otero,
Miguel A. Otero, Jr., A. G. Hood, and Charlie Keimle.
The first telephone line built in New Mexico was built
by the above-named directors between Las Vegas and
the Las Vegas Hot Springs. This was all done in the year
1880. The Las Vegas Telephone Company was organized
with Miguel A. Otero as President, and Miguel A. Otero,
Jr., Secretary and Treasurer. We put in an exchange under
A. G. Hood, General Manager. Miss Nellie Cummings took
charge of the switch-board, and I believe was first "Hello
Girl" in New Mexico; she held this position for some years,
until her marriage with Mr. Otto G. Schaefer on November
5th, 1884, when she was succeeded by Mrs. Anna B. Shout.

Many people were invited throughout the Territory to
assist in the ceremonies attending the completion of the first
railroad to enter Santa Fé, next to the oldest town in the
United States, and I was one of a party to represent Las
Vegas during this great event. The Atchison, Topeka &

Santa Fé Railroad reached this city on February 15th, 1880, and the occasion was celebrated by an excursion to the Missouri river in Pullman coaches, given complimentary by the railroad company through the New Mexico representatives, Governor George T. Anthony, Hon. Miguel A. Otero, and Hon. Henry L. Waldo to the 24th Legislative Assembly, then in session, other territorial officials and prominent business men throughout the Territory. The train was in charge of Major Thomas J. Anderson, the General Passenger Agent of the railroad, and visited Topeka, Lawrence, Kansas City, Atchison, and Leavenworth.

In the same year, 1880, on May 14th, the Albuquerque Street Railroad Company was incorporated, and cars were soon running, the first street railroad to be operated in New Mexico. A few months later, on December 20th, the Las Vegas Street Railway Company was incorporated, and cars commenced running shortly thereafter.

In an earlier chapter of this book I mention my uncle, Don Manuel A. Otero, and give a description of his home at La Constancia, Valencia County, and also our family's visit with him during the year 1872. He and my father were the last of the immediate family of my grandparents and were most devoted brothers. We were all greatly shocked at receiving a telegram from my cousin announcing the death of my Uncle Manuel which occurred at his home on Saturday, February 25th, 1882.

The Las Vegas *Daily Optic* of Monday, February 27th, had this mention of his death: "Another link that binds us to the past has been severed by the death at a ripe old age of Don Manuel A. Otero at La Constancia, Valencia County, on Saturday. The disease that carried him off was typhoid pneumonia. Don Manuel was an older brother of Don Miguel A. Otero, and the father of Mrs. Dr. Henriquez of this city. The deceased was surrounded by every comfort that heart could wish; he was an excellent man, kind, con-

siderate, thoughtful, and his life was singularly free from
the vices and follies of our common humanity. All respected
him for his many virtues. In the several spheres of husband,
father, and citizen, he occupied a position worthy of emula-
tion. One by one the old settlers are passing away. They will
all soon be gone."

Don Manuel was born on March 20th, 1815, and had
not quite reached the age of sixty-seven years.

My father was almost heartbroken over the death of his
only brother and never fully recovered from the shock. The
family had scarcely become reconciled over this death before
another one of the immediate family followed.

Don Ambrosio Armijo died in Albuquerque on Easter
Sunday, April 9th, 1882, at the age of 65 years. He was my
uncle by marriage, having married Maria Candelaria Otero,
my father's youngest sister, who preceded him to the grave.
They were the parents of five children, four of whom, Per-
fecto, Jesus, Mariano, and Mrs. Symington, survive them.

Don Ambrosio Armijo was well and favorably known
throughout New Mexico. He was born at Ranchos de Albuquerque in 1817, and was a most useful citizen to the community in which he resided, as well as one of the most
prominent men in the Territory. Before the advent of the
railroad into New Mexico, Don Ambrosio Armijo owned
and operated one of the largest mule trains carrying freight
across the plains from the end of the railroad to points in
New Mexico. While he never accompanied the outfit himself, it was always in charge of one of his sons. He was a
large property owner and besides conducted one of the
largest mercantile establishments in Old Albuquerque.

Just at this time great preparations were being made for
the opening of the Montezuma Hotel at the Las Vegas Hot
Springs by the Atchison, Topeka & Santa Fé Railroad.
The day had been set and elaborate invitations were sent
out for April 17th, 1882. The directors of the railroad held

a meeting in the morning at Santa Fé, and my father was
again elected Vice-President of the New Mexico and Southern Pacific Railroad. After the adjournment of the meeting
they all came over on a special train to participate in the
opening of the hotel. At the banquet and reception Colonel
W. G. Dickinson of Topeka, Kans., was the master of ceremonies. Don Miguel A. Otero, my father, was called upon
to respond to the toast, *Railroads as a Civilizer*. In being
introduced, Don Miguel was mentioned as a man whose
name is familiar to everyone who is at all acquainted with
the history of New Mexico. After making his salutation, he
proceeded in the following classic language:

"I cannot better express my feelings on this auspicious occasion,
and in the presence of this brilliant assemblage, than by relating
the beautiful and pathetic superstition of the Pecos Indians, whose
home, for ages, had been in the valley contiguous to that in which
we meet tonight. These brave and simple-minded people implicitly
believed that their mighty but ill-fated emperor, the glorious Montezuma, disappeared from view amid the clouds of their native
mountains, that he promised to return to his adoring people once
more, after ages had passed away. With trusting faith they believed
his words; and he promised when the day of his return arrived
that he would come in glory from the east — his face bright and
fair as the noonday sun, and clad in all the garments of glory.
Century after century passed away but still they kept alive their
sacred fire, which burned as brightly as their undying faith, but at
length the fire in their temple and their faith died out. The last
remnant of the faithful old tribe has disappeared from the homes of
their fathers and the ancient shrine is in ruins, but we, who fill their
places, have lived to see the return of the mighty chieftain. With
power and majesty he comes, with the ancient sun-god from the
east, and tonight we hail his coming in the new and splendid halls
of the Montezuma!

After the banquet the spacious dining hall was cleared of
its tables and the floor prepared for the dance. At 9:30 Prof.
Helm's famous Fourth Cavalry orchestra sounded the grand

march and the ball was inaugurated under most favorable auspices.

There were fourteen dances on the program, which kept the "light fantastic" feet in a bustle till eight in the morning. It was one of the grandest affairs ever given in New Mexico up to that time.

About three weeks after the opening of the Montezuma Hotel, as above related, my father was busily engaged in pushing the work of building the branch railroad from the town of Bernalillo, now the county seat of Sandoval County, to the Jemez Hot Springs, and he was already planning for an excursion, to be made from Las Vegas, Santa Fé and Albuquerque to celebrate the opening of the new hotel at the Springs. At this time the hotel was almost completed and ready for furnishing. About the middle of the month of May my father returned to Las Vegas. While there he met his old friend, J. M. Studebaker, who had just arrived from South Bend, Ind. Stopping at the Hot Springs at this time was another old friend, Michael Spangler, sheriff of Arapahoe County, Colo. They were both anxious for a fishing trip into the mountains, so my father arranged to have me take them out, as he had to return at once to the Jemez Hot Springs. I quickly arranged the details, and the following morning after my father's departure south, we started out with every intention of staying for at least a couple of weeks in the mountains. In our outfit we had two covered wagons and complete camping and fishing equipment and two extra men; one to cook and the other to take care of the camp, look after the horses and attend to all the chores. I rode my saddle pony, Kiowa, while Alex Savajeau took his horse and accompanied me on horseback. In the party were J. M. Studebaker, Michael Spangler, R. J. Holmes, Alex Savajeau, myself and the two men servants.

Late that same afternoon we were camped on a beautiful stream where the speckled beauties were very plentiful, we having caught, in a few minutes, sufficient trout for our supper. We were tired and went to bed soon after eating. The next morning we all started out long before sunrise and returned for breakfast about ten o'clock with our baskets filled with good-sized trout.

Almost immediately after eating my breakfast a queer sensation came over me, something like a premonition which seemed to be calling me home. Finally I could stand it no longer and reluctantly told Mr. Studebaker, and at the same time advised him that my action need not interfere with the party as I would take Kiowa and ride back alone. They, however, would not listen to such a proposition on my part, all of them insisting upon going with me. We reached Las Vegas late that same afternoon and the first man I met was Harry W. Kelly, who asked me if I had been home, saying: "Your father, Don Miguel, is a very sick man; he arrived this morning from the Jemez Hot Springs, on a special train from Bernalillo." I went immediately to our home and found my father very low with an attack of pneumonia. He seemed greatly relieved when he saw me enter the room and said he wanted to have a talk with me, but Doctor Gordon thought I had better wait until the next day. The following morning he complained of feeling cold, and he called to us boys, Page and myself, to go down to Houghton's Hardware Store and bring back a couple of oil burning stoves to put in his room. He got up and walked into my sister's room and got into her bed, saying, "It is too cold in that room." We left him talking to my mother and Judge John F. Bostwick, his attorney, who was joking with him about being sick.

Just as we had selected the stoves and were in the act of leaving Houghton's store with them, Judge Bostwick appeared at the door and said: "Boys, leave the stoves; it is all over with Don Miguel; he died just as you were leaving the house." It happened to be Decoration Day, May 30, 1882.

The news of my father's death spread rapidly over both

the Old and New Towns and people called by the hundreds. The entire Territory was in mourning and telegrams poured in from all over New Mexico and much of the western country.

The first part of the year 1882 in New Mexico had rather a heavy death toll among the prominent old settlers, as Don Manuel A. Otero, Don Ambrosio Armijo and Don Miguel A. Otero all died within ninety days' time.

Our family burial place being in Riverside cemetery, Denver, Colo., where my sister Gertrude is buried, we decided to bury my father there. The Atchison, Topeka & Santa Fé Railroad officials placed a fully equipped train at our disposal for the family and those friends who wished to attend the funeral at Denver, and hundreds went with us from all parts of the Territory.

On June 2nd the Denver *Press* sent out the following telegram to the *Daily Optic:*

THE OTERO OBSEQUIES

The Last Sad Rites Conducted With Great Ceremony

The funeral services of Don Miguel A. Otero are now begun, with the preparations of the most elaborate order. The Denver lodges of Free Masons have charge of the obsequies and inter the remains with all the beautiful ceremonies of the mystic order. The weather is threatening rain but nevertheless Trinity Memorial Church is well filled with the most prominent people of Colorado, including Governor Pitkin, all the state officials in a body, and a large number of prominent railroad officials.

The floral decorations are very beautiful and appropriate about the altar. The casket is covered with wreaths and festoons, and in the center are the words "Rest" in immortelles. Beneath is the silver plate bearing the simple inscription of the deceased's name, with the date of his birth and death.

The remains are fairly preserved but are not opened to view today.

Rev. Charles H. Marshall preaches the funeral sermon and by the hour *The Optic* goes to press this evening, New Mexico's greatest son will be lying in Riverside, in the vault by the side of his lost daughter Gertie. Miss Mamie, the only surviving daughter, reaches Kansas City this evening, and will arrive in Denver tomorrow night.

THE TRIBUTE OF THE PRESS.

The *Republican* and the *Rocky Mountain News,* of this morning, devote much space editorially to the memory of the late lamented Don Miguel. Other papers yet to issue will contain tributes of respect to the memory of the mighty fallen.

The bereaved Otero family and party of Las Vegas friends return home on Monday.

Tne *Daily Optic* of June 2nd says editorially:

The well-written obituaries of the late Don Miguel A. Otero, which have appeared, would fill a large sized scrap book, and he deserved every word of eulogy passed upon him. Such men as he do not exist in every community, and such men as he are seldom appreciated until after the dread summons have been served upon them.

I feel that this chapter devoted so largely to the close of my father's long and useful career would not be complete without a biographical sketch which will give in conspectus the outstanding events in his life. While doing this involves some slight repetition of what appears here and there in the book, I believe it gains in weight to be assembled in one place and to be enlarged with some additional material.

Don Miguel Antonio Otero (I), was born at Valencia, County of Valencia, Territory of New Mexico (at that time a province of Old Mexico), on June 21st, 1829, and was the youngest child of Don Vicente Otero and Doña Gertrudes Chaves y Aragon.

He was first sent to a private school at Valencia, conducted by a Catholic priest, where he remained until he was eleven years of age, learning the rudiments of Spanish, arithmetic and religion. In 1841 he went to the St. Louis University at St. Louis, and remained there until the Mexican War broke out in 1846, when he was recalled home by his parents. In the spring of 1847 he was sent of his own choice and at his own request to Pingree's College at Fishkill on the Hudson, New York. His father gave him his own choice of many schools which had been recommended, and he chose a Protestant institution so as to acquaint himself with the difference between the two ruling religions; the Roman Catholic and the Protestant. His mother had destined him for the priesthood, but the two years' attendance at the Pingree College liberalized his views without changing his religion.

At the Pingree College he became a Professor on the Faculty and was made Assistant Professor of Latin and Greek. He was a very studious young man, worked constantly with his books, and soon was made Assistant to the Principal of the College, a great honor for one of his age. This position he held for a term of two years, and to the entire satisfaction of the Principal. His school and college life covered a period of twelve years. Under the advice of the Principal of the Pingree College he took up the study of law. He first began his studies in the office of Hon. James Thayer, a distinguished lawyer of the State of New York, who was at that time living in Fishkill. This was in the year 1849. In the winter of 1849-1850 he went to New York City and entered the law office of General Sanford, remaining there one year, at the end of which time he decided to return to St. Louis, where he at once entered the law office of Hon. Trusten Polk, who was afterwards elected Governor of and still later United States Senator from Missouri. He completed his studies in his office, was admitted to the bar of the State of Missouri early in the spring of 1852, and at once took out his license to practice in that state.

BIBLIOGRAPHY

BIBLIOGRAPHY

Books in English

Acuña, Rudolph. Story of the Mexican Americans: The Men and The Land.
New York: American Book Co., 1970.

Bancroft, Hubert House. California Pastoral 1769-1848. San Francisco:
The History Co., 1888.

Beck, Warren. New Mexico: A History of Four Centuries. Norman:
Oklahoma University Press, 1962.

Bentley, Harold. A Dictionary of Spanish Terms in English with Special
Reference to the American Southwest. New York: Columbia University Press, 1932.

Bernstein, Harry. Making of an Inter-American Mind. Gainesville: University of Florida Press, 1961.

————, Origins of Inter-American Interest, 1700-1812. Philadelphia,
University of Pennsylvania Press, 1945.

Bishop, Morris. The Odyssey of Cabeza de Vaca. New York & London:
The Century Co., 1933.

Blackmar, Frank Wilson. Spanish Colonization in the Southwest. Baltimore: Johns Hopkins University Press, 1890.

Bogardus, Emory S. The Mexican in the United States. Los Angeles: University of Southern California, 1934.

Bolton, Herbert E. Coronado, Knight of Pueblos and Plains. New York:
Withlesey House, 1949.

————. Spanish Exploration in the Southwest, 1542-1706. New York:
1916.

————. Texas in the Middle Eighteenth Century, Studies in Spanish Colonial History and Administration. New York: Russell & Russell, 1962.

————. The Spanish Borderlands. A Chronicle of Florida and the Southwest. New Haven: Yale University Press, 1921.

Bolton, Herbert E. and Thomas M. Marshall. The Colonization of North
   America 1492-1783. New York: Macmillan Co., 1920.

Bourne, Edward G. Spain in America. 1450-1580. New York & London,
   1904.

Burma, John H., ed. Mexican-Americans in the United States. Cambridge,
   Mass.: Schenkman Publishing Co., 1970.

─────────. Spanish-Speaking Groups in the United States. Durham, N.C.:
   Duke University Press, 1954.

Campa, Arthur L. Spanish Folk-Poetry in New Mexico. Albuquerque:
   University of New Mexico Press, 1946.

Castro, Tony. Chicano Power: The Emergence of Mexican America. New
   York: Saturday Review Press, 1974.

Chapman, C.E. The Founding of Spanish California. New York: Macmillan Co., 1916.

Chenault, Lawrence. The Puerto Rican Migrant in New York City. New
   York: Columbia University Press, 1938.

Cook, Warren L. Flood Tide of Empire: Spain and the Pacific Northwest,
   1543-1819. New Haven & London: Yale University Press, 1973.

Cordasco, Francesco and Eugene Bucchioni. The Puerto Rican Experience.
   Totowa, N.J.: Rowman & Littlefield, 1973.

Cunningham Graham, R.B. Hernando de Soto. New York: Dial Press,
   1924.

de Cárdenas, Juan Francisco. Hispanic Culture and Language in the United
   States. New York: Hispanic Institute.

De Onís, José. The United States as Seen by Spanish American Writers,
   1776-1890. New York: Hispanic Institute, 1952.

De Onís, Juan, ed. & trans. The America of José Martí. New York: Funk
   & Wagnalls, 1954.

Del Río, Angel. The Clash & Attraction of Two Cultures. The Hispanic
   and Anglo-Saxon Worlds in America. Trans. and ed. James F. Shearer.
   Baton Rouge: Louisiana State University Press, 1965.

Dunne, Peter Masten. Black Robes in Lower California. Berkeley: University of California Press, 1952.

Fernández-Flores, Darío. The Spanish Heritage in the United States. Madrid: Publicaciones Españolas, 1971.

Fitzpatrick, Joseph P. Puerto Rican Americans: The Meaning of Migration to the Mainland. Englewood Cliffs, N.J.: Prentice-Hall, 1971.

Gamio, Manuel. Mexican Immigration to the United States; A Study of Human Migration and Adjustment. Chicago: University of Chicago Press, 1930.

Grebler, Leo. The Mexican American People, The Nation's Second Largest Minority. New York: The Free Press, 1970.

Hammon, George Peter. The Rediscovery of New Mexico 1580-1594. Albuquerque: University of New Mexico Press, 1966.

Heizer, Robert F. and Alan J. Almquist. The Other Californians. Berkeley: University of California Press, 1971.

Horgan, Paul. Conquistadores in North American History. New York: Farrar, Strauss & Co., 1963.

Jones, Oakah L. Pueblo Warriors & Spanish Conquest. Norman: University of Oklahoma Press, 1966.

Kibbe, Pauline R. Latin Americans in Texas. Albuquerque: University of New Mexico Press, 1946.

Kirkpatrick, Fredrick Alexander. The Spanish Conquistadores. Cleveland: World Publishing Co., 1962.

Kubler, George. The Religious Architecture of New Mexico in the Colonial Period and Since the American Occupation. Colorado Springs: The Taylor Museum, 1940.

Lea, Aurora Lucero-White. Folklore of the Hispanic Southwest. San Antonio, Texas: The Naylor Co., 1953.

Leonard, P.H. The Decline of the Californias: A Social History of the Spanish-Speaking Californias, 1846-1890. Berkeley: University of California Press, 1966.

Lowery, Woodbury. The Spanish Settlements within the Present Limits of the United States 1513-1561. New York: Russell & Russell, 1959.

McWilliams, Carey. North from Mexico: The Spanish-Speaking People of the United States. New York: J.B. Lippincott, 1943.

Madsen, William. The Mexican Americans of South Texas. New York: 1964.

Mañach, Jorge. Martí: Apostle of Freedom. Trans. Coley Taylor. New York: Devin-Adair, 1960.

Mapps, Edward. Puerto Rican Perspectives. Metuchen, N.J.: The Scarecrow Press, 1974.

Meier, Matt. S. & Feliciano Rivera. The Chicanos. New York: Hill & Wang, 1972.

Mixon, Ada. De Soto's Route West of Mississippi. New York: American Historical Society, 1918.

Monaghan, Jay. Chile, Peru and the California Gold Rush of 1849. Berkeley: University of California Press, 1973.

Moore, Joan W. with Alfred Cuéllar. Mexican Americans. Englewood Cliffs, N.J.: Prentice Hall, 1970.

Moquín, Wayne and Charles Van Doren, eds. A Documentary History of the Mexican Americans. New York: Praeger, 1971.

Nasatir, Abraham Phineas. Spanish War Vessels on the Mississippi 1792-1796. New Haven: Yale University Press, 1968.

Newton, Clarke. Famous Mexican-Americans. New York: Dodd, Mead, 1972.

Nogales, Luis G. The Mexican-American, a Selected and Annotated Bibliography. Stanford University, 1971.

Palacios, Arturo, ed. The Mexican-American Directory. Washington, D.C.: Executive Systems Corp., 1969.

Priestly, Herbert Ingram. The Coming of the White Man, 1492-1848. New York: Macmillan Co., 1929.

Rippy, James Fred. Rivalry of the United States and Great Britain over Latin America (1808-1830). Baltimore: Johns Hopkins Press, 1929.

Sánchez, George. Forgotten People: A Study of New Mexicans. Albuquerque: University of New Mexico Press, 1940.

Senior, Clarence. The Puerto Ricans, Strangers-Then Neighbors. Chicago: Quadrangle Books, 1965.

Servín, Manuel Patricio, ed. The Mexican-Americans: An Awakening Minority. Beverly Hills: Glencoe Publishing, 1970.

Sexton, R. Spanish Influence on American Architecture and Decoration. New York: Bretano, 1927.

Silverberg, Robert. The Pueblo Revolt. New York: Weybright & Talley, 1970.

Simmer, Edward. The Chicano: From Caricature to Self-Portrait. New York: New American Library, 1971.

Solien González, Nancie L. The Spanish-Americans of New Mexico: A Heritage of Pride. Albuquerque: University of New Mexico Press, 1969.

Steiner, Stan. The Mexican Americans. New York: Harper & Row, Inc., 1969.

Wagner, H.R. Juan Rodríguez Cabrillo, Discoverer of California. San Francisco: 1941.

Whitaker, A.P. Latin America and the Enlightenment. New York: Appleton Publishing Co., 1942.

————. The Spanish American Frontier: 1783-1795. The Westward Movement and the Spanish Retreat in the Mississippi Valley. Gloucester, Mass.: Peter Smith, 1962.

Wright, James Leitch. Anglo-Spanish Rivalry in North America. Athens: University of Georgia Press, 1971.

Articles in English

Althus, William D. "The American Mexican: The Survival of a Culture," Journal of Social Psychology, XXIX (May, 1949), 211-220.

Altrocchi, J.C. "San Francisco's Spanish Beginnings," Catholic World, 169 (April, 1949), 13-20.

Alvarez, José Hernández, "A Demographic Profile of the Mexican Immigration to the United States, 1910-1950," Journal of International Studies, 8 (July, 1966), 471-496.

Amaral, José Vásquez, "Hispanic Culture Makes its Mark in New York," Américas, 16 (January, 1964).

Bernstein, Harry. "Spanish Influences in the United States-Economic Aspects," Hispanic American Historical Review, XVIII (February, 1938).

Bolton, H. E. "The Spanish Occupation of Texas," South Western Historical Quarterly, XVI (July, 1912).

Brown, Vera Lee. "Anglo-Spanish Relations in the Closing Years of the Colonial Era," Hispanic American Historical Review, V, 1922.

Dillard, J. L. "The Lingua Franca in the American Southwest," Revista Interamericana, III, 3 (Fall, 1973), 278-289.

Gómez-Quiñones, Juan. "Towards a Perspective on Chicano History," Aztlán 2, 12 (Fall, 1971), 1-51.

Hackett, C. W. "The Delimitation of Political Jurisdiction in Spanish North America to 1535," The Hispanic American Historical Review, I (February, 1918), 40-69.

Helman, Edith F. "Early Interest in Spanish in New England, (1815-1835)," Hispania, (August, 1945), 339-351.

Jones, O. L. Jr. "The Conquest of California," Journal of the West, 5 (1966), 187-202.

Knowlton, Clark S. "The Spanish Americans in New Mexico," Sociology & Social Research, XLV (July, 1961).

Lloyd Miller, Thomas. "Mexican-Texans at the Alamo," Journal of Mexican American History, 11, i (Fall, 1971), 33-44.

Marcella, Gabriel, "Spanish-Mexican Contributions to the Southwest," Journal of Mexican American History, I (Fall, 1970), 1-16.

Mechan, J. L. "Northern Expansion of New Spain 1522-1822: A Selected Descriptive Bibliographical List," Hispanic American Historical Review, VII (1927), 233-276.

Morefield, Richard Henry, "Mexicans in the California Mines, 1848-1853," California Historical Society Quarterly, XXXV (March, 1956), 37-46.

Patee, Richard. "The Puerto Ricans," Annals of the American Academy of Political and Social Science, CCXXIII (September, 1942), 49-54.

Reynolds, Russell, "Spanish Law Influence in Louisiana," Hispania, 56, 4(December, 1973), 1076-1082.

Robinson, Cecil. "Spring Water with a Taste of the Land; The Mexican Presence in the American Southwest," American West, 3 (Summer, 1966), 6-15.

Romano, Octavia Ignacio, "The Historical & Intellectual Presence of Mexican Americans," El Grito, 11 (Winter, 1969), 32-47.

Spell, J.R. "An Illustrious Spaniard in Philadelphia," Hispanic Review, IV, 1936, 136-140.

Vaca, Nick C. "The Mexican-American in the Social Sciences 1912-1970, part II 1936-1970," El Grito, IV, i (Fall, 1970), 52-65.

Wallis, Wilson D. "The Mexican Immigrant of California," Pacific Review, II (December, 1921), 444-454.

Wright, Irene A. "Spanish Policy toward Virginia, 1606-1612," American Historical Review, XXV (1920).

Zegrí, Armando. "Spanish Americans Invade Broadway," Américas, 10 (November, 1958), 26-30.

Doctoral Dissertations

Bowan, Jean Donald. "The Spanish of San Antonio, New Mexico." University of Texas, 1960.

Romano, Octavio. "Don Pedrito Jaramillo: The Emergence of a Mexican-American Folk Saint." University of California, 1964.

Simmons, Marc Steven. "Spanish Government in New Mexico at the End of the Colonial Period." University of New Mexico, 1965.

Stimson, F.S. "Spanish Themes in Early American Literature in Novels, Drama and Verse, 1770-1830." University of Michigan,

Swadesh, Frances León. "Hispanic Americans of the Ute Frontier from the Chama Valley to the San Juan Basin, 1694-1960." University of Colorado,

Books in Spanish

Altamira, Rafael. La huella de España en América. Madrid: 1924.

Babín, María Teresa. Panorama de la cultura puertorriqueña. New York: Las Americas Publishing Co., 1958.

Barrenechea, Ana María & Beatriz Lavandera. Domingo Faustino Sarmiento. Buenos Aires: Centro Editor de América Latina, 1967.

Bayle, Constantino. España en Indias. Madrid: Editorial Nacional, 1944.

Conrotte, Manuel. La intervención de España en la independencia de los Estados Unidos de la América del Norte. Madrid: V. Suárez, 1920.

De Onís, Federico. España en América. San Juan, P.R.: 1955.

Fernández, Juan Romulo. Sarmiento, semblanza e inconografía. Buenos Aires: Librería del Colegio, 1938.

Fernández-Flores, Darío. Drama y aventura de los españoles en Florida. Madrid: Ediciones de Cultura Hispánica, 1963.

Fernández-Shaw, Carlos. Presencia española en los Estados Unidos. Madrid: Colección Historia.

Folgelquist, Donald F. Españoles de América y americanos de España. Madrid: Editorial Aguilar, 1970.

García Mercadal, José. Lo que España llevó a América. Madrid: Taurus, 1959.

Garrigues, Emilio. Los españoles en la otra América. Madrid: Ediciones Cultura Hispánica, 1965.

Gil Munilla, Octavio. Participación de España en la génesis histórica de los Estados Unidos. Madrid: Publicaciones Españolas, 1963.

Majo Framis, Ricardo. Vida y hechos de Fray Junípero Serra, fundador de la nueva California. Madrid: Espasa-Calpe, 1956.

Morales Padrón, Francisco. Historia del descubrimiento y conquista de América. Madrid: Editora Nacional, 1963.

————. Participación de España en la independencia política de los Estados Unidos. Madrid: Publicaciones Españolas, 1963.

Peñuelas, Marcelino C. Lo español en el sureste de los Estados Unidos. Madrid: Ediciones Cultura Hispánica, 1964.

Pereyra, Carlos. La obra de España en América. Madrid: 1920.

Rodríguez Casado, Vicente. Primeros años de dominación española en la Luisiana. Madrid: 1942.

Romera Navarro, M. El hispanismo en Norteamérica. Madrid: Editorial Renacimiento, 1917.

Sanz y Díaz, José. Fray Junípero Serra, fundador de California. Madrid: Publicaciones Espanolas, 1963.

Thompson, Buchanan Parker. La ayuda española en la guerra de la independencia norteamericana. Madrid: 1961.

Urdapilleta, Antonio. Andanzas y desventuras de Alvar Núñez Cabeza de Vaca. Madrid: 1949.

Urrutia, Francisco José. Los Estados Unidos de América y las repúblicas hispano-americanas de 1810-1830. Madrid: Biblioteca Ayacucho, 1918.

Williams, Stanley Thomas. La huella española en la literatura norteamericana. Madrid: Editorial Gredos, 1957.

Zea, Leopoldo. Latinoamérica y el mundo. Caracas: Universidad Central de Venezuela, 1960.

Articles in Spanish

Anderson Imbert, Enrique. "Domingo Faustino Sarmiento, " Américas, XXIV, núm. 2 (febrero, 1972), S6-S11.

Baiocco, C.N. "Literatura española de Washington Irving, " Américas, XXIV, núm. 4 (abril, 1972), 2-12.

Bernstein, Harry. "Las primeras relaciones intelectuales entre New England y el mundo hispánico, 1700-1815, " Revista Hispánica Moderna, V (1939), 1-17.

Cano, J.L. "Juan Ramón Jiménez y la poesía norteamericana, " Revista Shell, año 7, (septiembre, 1958), 35-38.

del Río, Angel. "Choque y atracción de dos culturas, el mundo hispánico y el mundo anglo-sajón, " Ibérica, IX, núms. 1-3, 1961, (núm.1, pags. 8-11; núm 2, pags. 8-16; núm. 3, pags. 9-11).

Gonzales, M.P. "Las relaciones intelectuales entre los Estados Unidos e Hispanoamérica, " Universidad de la Habana, año VII, núms. 24-25,

Salas, Irma S. "Las relaciones culturales entre Chile y los Estados Unidos, " Boletín de la Unión Panamericana, 1940, 57-576.

Ureña, Henríquez, "España en la cultura moderna, " Yelmo (Madrid), 3 (diciembre-enero, 1971-72), 41-43.

Zavala, Silvio. "Etapa de recepcion de influencias y eclecticismo en la cultura colonial de América, " Revista Hispánica Moderna, año XXXL (enero-octubre, 1965), 450-454.

NAME INDEX